Jasper Green Pkennington

Vincit amor patriae.

CLIFFORD P. MOREHOUSE

A Layman
Looks
at the Church

NEW YORK

1964

ACKNOWLEDGMENTS

Grateful acknowledgment is made to the following publishers, authors, and agents for permission to use material from the titles listed:

Atlantic Monthly—Barbara Ward, "The Quest for Christian Unity," *Atlantic,* August, 1962.

Christian Century Foundation—Martin Luther King, Jr., excerpt from "Letter from Birmingham Jail" from June 12, 1963 issue of *The Christian Century.* Copyright 1963. Reprinted by permission.

Gardiner M. Day, paragraph from his sermon on War and Peace, May 26, 1963.

The Episcopalian—Louis Cassel, "What About Communism in Our Churches," July, 1961 issue of *The Episcopalian.*

Forward Movement Publications—excerpt from *Laymen Look at the Laity.* Reprinted by permission.

Harper & Row, Publishers—Arnold Rose, for postscript which appears in *An American Dilemma* by Gunnar Myrdal. Reprinted by permission.

Life—Excerpts from Editorial Page of December 14, 1962 issue of *Life.* Reprinted by permission.

Morehouse-Barlow Co.—Theodore O. Wedel, *Modern Canterbury Pilgrims.* Reprinted by permission.

National Council of the Churches of Christ—Quoted from *A Christian's Handbook on Communism.* Published by the National Council of Churches. Copyright 1962. Used with permission.

Seabury Press—C. B. Moss, *The Christian Faith.* Copyright by S.P.C.K.

S.P.C.K.—Michael Ramsey, *Image Old and New.* Published in the U.S.A. by Forward Movement Publications, 1963.

Annie Laurie Williams, Agent—Alan Paton, "Meditation for a Young Boy Confirmed." Copyright 1954 by Alan Paton.

Preface

THIS is a book that has been, in a sense, thirty years in the writing. I am a layman, and I hope I think and write as a layman. But I have had a unique opportunity to observe the Church at work at all levels, from the parochial to the international, from the denominational (though I dislike the word) to the ecumenical. The substance of many of the chapters has been given in the form of addresses to diocesan conventions, Church conferences, and interdenominational meetings. Some have been published, in slightly different form, in such periodicals as *The Episcopalian, The Living Church,* and *American Church News.* I am grateful for their permission to reprint material that they have originally published, even when revised out of all semblance to the original.

I write as a communicant of the Episcopal Church and a member of the Church universal. If much of what I have written reveals its Anglican origin and appears to be addressed primarily to Episcopalians, nevertheless I hope it will have some appeal to members of other Christian bodies, both Catholic and Protestant, for many of our problems are similar; and in the new "ecumenical dialogue," it is well for members of each communion to see how things look from the viewpoint of one who observes them from a different background.

I am greatly indebted to Kay Smallzried of the Morehouse-Barlow editorial staff, and to the editors of Seabury Press and the Episcopal Book Club for their editorial assistance, and to my faithful secretary, Margaret Wiener, for many hours of typing "above and beyond the call of duty."

CLIFFORD P. MOREHOUSE

Table of Contents

Chapter

Preface   v

1. What Can We Believe?   3

2. What Is the Church?   14

3. The Role of the Laity   24

4. Bishops and Priests   31

5. The World Is My Parish   40

6. "Dig We Must"   54

7. The General Convention   66

8. What about Christian Unity?   77

9. Ecumenical Conferences and Conversations   89

10. The Anglican Communion and Mission   101

11. The Christian Family   111

12. Communism and Anti-Communism   125

13. War and Peace   136

14. The Church and Segregation   144

15. The Church Looks to the Future   156

16. The Church's Secret Weapon   167

Notes   179

A Layman
Looks
at the Church

What Can We Believe?

CHAPTER ONE

CHURCH attendance in the United States today is, we are told, greater than ever in our history. If one were making lists of "good" and "bad" things, the matter of church attendance would, I suppose, go under the heading "good" things. I wonder, however, whether it really indicates depth of spiritual conviction, or whether in many cases it simply reflects social custom.

Why do people go to church? Many go for the right reason— to worship God; others to secure peace of mind; and still others just because it is the thing to do.

It is logical also to assume that these people who go to church believe in God. And if they profess and call themselves Christians, they believe in Jesus Christ also. But, perhaps, there is a catch in that word *also*. Do they really recognize our Lord as the Son of God? And if they do, what difference does it make to them?

Having raised such rhetorical questions, let's drop the word "they" and start speaking about ourselves. Most of the readers of this book do not hesitate to stand with the congregation on Sunday and recite boldly: "I believe in one God the Father Almighty, Maker of heaven and earth, And of all things visible and invisible."

Stop right here. Who is this God in whom we so easily proclaim our faith? Is he a remote, impersonal creator? Is he some vague personality "up there" or "out yonder"? Is he a stern and relentless judge? A latter-day Neptune who rules wind and wave, storm and tempest? Or is he a personal being whom we can know and love, and who loves us?

Don't be too sure you can give a ready answer. The Bishop of Woolwich, in his controversial book *Honest to God*[1] claims that the

Bible speaks of a God who is "up there" or "out yonder"; and he says: "Every one of us lives with some mental picture of a God 'out there,' a God who exists above and beyond the world he made, a God to whom we pray and to whom we go when we die." The Bishop, however, has outgrown this concept of God, and he appears to think that we should throw the traditional idea of religion into the "hell box" and start over. He explicitly says, "The first thing we must be ready to let go is our image of God himself."

I think that the Bishop is a century behind the times. No intelligent person whom I know thinks of God as a person "up there" or "out yonder," looking down benevolently upon the world he created and meddling with it from time to time to see that it goes according to his plan. In fact, I am inclined to agree with the English scholar who, in an effective reply to the Bishop's book—a book which has upset the faith of so many laymen on both sides of the Atlantic—observed that much of what the Bishop wrote in *Honest to God* is "not heresy, but just nonsense." [2]

To answer the question about what we mean by God when we stand and pledge allegiance to him in the Creed, we have only to turn to the Prayer Book Offices of Instruction:

Question. What do you chiefly learn in these Articles of your Belief?
Answer. First, I learn to believe in God the Father, who hath made me, and all the world.
Secondly, in God the Son, who hath redeemed me, and all mankind.
Thirdly, in God the Holy Ghost, who sanctifieth me, and all the people of God.

This is the doctrine of the Holy Trinity. It tells us, insofar as can be done in human words, who God is and what he is like. It does not tell us where he is, for that is a matter with which Christians need not be unduly concerned. Certainly God is "up there" and "out yonder," but he is also "down here" and "inside."

There are many ways in which we may learn about God and, better yet, come to know him. For knowing *about* a person is not the same as knowing him personally; recognizing the existence of someone is never the same as loving him and being loved by him. That is true in human relationships. It is also true in the human-divine relationship. We can know about God, and we can know him. We can love him, and know ourselves to be loved by him.

"The knowledge and love of God," however, is not something that comes without effort—at least, to adults. Children, almost instinctively, seem able to know God and love him, because they have not yet come up against the doubts and perplexities, the trials and troubles that beset adults, nor the sins that separate the human soul from God. Bishop Lewis, of Olympia, writing to his clergy, put it quite simply: "So often our doubts and uncertainties are only a cheap mixture of ignorance and mental laziness." He might have added, "and of the sin of pride, which centers attention on self instead of God."

We can learn much about God just by keeping our eyes and ears open and by observing the universe which he has created. The universe is one of order, of cause and effect, of interdependence in nature. The world in which we live is a planet unlike any other which astronomers so far have observed (though by God's law of probabilities there are probably others), and one so delicately adjusted that plant, animal, and human life are possible. The human body is wonderfully constructed to cope with its environment and to reproduce its kind. The human mind is even more wonderful, for it can bend nature to its own purposes; it is creative and hence man may learn, reflect, and share in God's work of creation. That is what the Old Testament means by saying that God made man in his own image—not that man looks like God, or that God is a sort of superman, but that through the power of creativity in man God reveals something of his nature.

We can also learn about God by reading the Bible, the age-old record of God's dealings with his people. There we discover something quite astonishing: that as man through the ages has sought God, so God through the ages has sought man and has revealed himself gradually to those who respond to his seeking. God's self-revelation has been carefully measured to the spiritual perception of man at each stage of mankind's understanding and civilization. He first revealed himself as the God of power and terrible majesty—the God of the thunder and lightning, of storm and tempest and fire. Later he revealed himself as the God of protection, so that the Israelites came to think of themselves as his chosen people. Still later, he revealed himself as the God of justice and impartiality, One who let the rains fall on the just and the unjust, and who visited the sins of the fathers upon the children, even to the third and fourth generation. Later yet, through the great prophets of the Old Testament, he revealed himself as the God of mercy and forgiveness, and, what is more important, as the God of love.

At last, in the fullness of time, he revealed himself in the Person of Jesus Christ his Son: God-made-man in order that man might *know* God, not just know about him, but know him personally. In Jesus' teachings, in his miracles, and above all in his day-to-day life, men saw God at work in their own lives, in their own small part of God's universe. They learned from this experience that God is love, and that his relationship to mankind is that of the loving Father.

Knowledge of God comes not only from the written word, for then we should still only know *about* him in an academic sort of way. So that we might truly know God, Jesus taught us to pray—not just publicly and formally (for the prophets did that), but also secretly, privately, in our own hearts, as simply and as intimately as a son talks with his father. And he taught us to expect from him the same kind of understanding response that a loving father gives.

Even more significant, God showed us how we might intimately share in his very life. "For in the night in which he was betrayed [what a dramatic choice of timing!] he took Bread; and when he had given thanks, he brake it and gave it to his disciples saying, Take, eat, this is my Body which is given for you; . . . Likewise, after supper, he took the Cup [of wine], and gave it to them saying:

. . . This is my Blood . . . which is shed for you . . . Do this, as oft as ye shall drink it, in remembrance of me."

Twenty-four hours later, his human body was nailed to the cross and his Blood was shed just as he had foretold at the Last Supper. The sins of mankind, yours and mine, as well as those of the priests, and the governor, and the soldiers, and the mob, had accomplished the death of the Son of God.

But that was not the end. On the third day he rose again and revealed himself anew to his followers. God's enemies are vanquished. The arrogant enemies of love fall before the arresting news that "God so loved the world that he gave his only begotten Son, to the end that all who believe in him should not perish, but have everlasting life." Death, which had been the end, the enemy of life, becomes an aspect of eternity. And when the Son returned to his Father, he sent the Holy Spirit into the Church and the world, to the end of the earth, to the time which has no end. These three are one God—Father, Son, and Holy Spirit.

Two thousand years later God is still with us and in exactly the way that he promised. We can still talk with him in prayer, and if we listen we can still hear his answer to our prayers. Best of all, in the Blessed Sacrament, the Holy Communion, we receive his Body and his Blood; we share in the power of his mighty resurrection and his glorious ascension; and we receive power to live as the children of the living and loving God.

That, briefly, is the faith by which we live. The faith of the Christian Church is not a set of arbitrary propositions; it is not based on theory or a set of hypotheses. It is the direct result of the teaching and example of our Lord, the faith of two thousand years of Christian experience. It is a way of life, stemming from our Lord's words: "I am the way, the truth, and the life." Those who follow in the way and live the life are given an increasing participation in the truth. They do not just know *about* God, they *know* God in prayer and sacrament, and through the guidance of the Holy Spirit in their very beings. They no longer think of God as a stranger, or as one whose existence must be proved through scholastic argument or test tube. They know him as a loving Father; they live in him and he in them; they know him through their own experience, quite as truly as those who saw him walking the rugged hills and dusty roads of ancient Palestine. Faith opens their spiritual eyes; teaching and experience blossom into the joyful recognition: I know that my Redeemer lives!

Faith is not only intensely personal, a fact of life and individual perception, it is also corporate. No man can be a Christian all by himself. Christianity is basically a corporate faith; and the corporate life of Christianity is witnessed by and through the holy Catholic Church. The Church is described by a variety of metaphors: Christ is the vine, and we are the branches; as the bride of Christ; as the path of righteousness; and, above all, as the Body of Christ, of which he is the Head and we are the members—"the mystical body of all the faithful."

The faith of the Church is not vague and nebulous. It is firmly rooted and grounded in the teachings of its Head and in the sacramental life that he ordained for it. The essence of that faith in its historic setting is proclaimed by the Apostles' and Nicene Creeds. Its life is that of Baptism and Holy Communion, of prayer and sacrament, of repentance and forgiveness. Its task is the reconciliation of men with God, the redemption of the world. Its officers are the bishops and other clergy; its membership, the whole body of the people of God.

The Church, like its master, is in the world but not of the world. It is a divine organism, not a human organization. Because it is made up of human beings, it suffers, in any age or among any people, from their frailties and weaknesses; yet it is always undergirded with the strength and perfection of its divine Lord; and before it is always his promise that the gates of hell shall not prevail against it.

There have always been some in the Church, even in high

places, who by their lack of faith deny our Lord even as St. Peter did at the time of Jesus' trial. There are also those who betray him as did Judas Iscariot. But St. Peter repented and became one of the greatest of the apostles; Judas, however, went out and hanged himself. Through the ages the Church has had among its leaders those whose doubts and denials wounded the Church, and those whose betrayal caused their own destruction. However, the doubts of one, the denials of another, even the betrayal of some, cannot cause the destruction of the Church, because the Church is greater than the sum of its members: it is the Body of Christ himself. And Christ has overcome doubt, denial, betrayal, and death!

It is sad when a bishop or priest of the Church confuses its members by expressing his own doubts and denials. The layman has a right to trust the bishops and other clergy, and to expect them to teach the faith of the Church rather than their own private opinions. He looks especially to the bishops to be the voice of authority in the Church. It is right that he should do so, for to them our Lord committed the keys of the kingdom. When a bishop makes a statement or publishes a book that casts doubt upon the essential doctrines of Christianity, or interprets them in such a way as to seem to deny them, he renders a great disservice to the laity, and he wounds the Body of Christ.

Anglicanism, with its strong tradition of intellectual freedom and its history of outstanding scholarship, sometimes seems to be particularly productive of public questionings, or denials. At the beginning of this chapter we noted a statement by a bishop who seemed to say that we should be so open-minded as to be prepared "to let go" our image of God himself. Actually, the bishop who declared that is a hard working and faithful shepherd of the sheep committed to his charge, and the book in question reveals a rare depth of faith and a vigorous sense of mission. He seems not to realize, however, that in his striving to reinterpret the faith he seems to deny it; and that the result is to drive away sincere men and women who look to him for the proper leadership and authority.

At his consecration a bishop-elect declares himself "ready, with all faithful diligence, to banish and drive away from the Church all erroneous and strange doctrine contrary to God's Word, and both privately and openly to call upon and encourage others to do the same." That is a solemn promise, one that cannot be made without absolute sincerity.

Recently I received a letter from a layman who cited several recent statements and publications by bishops that seemed to cast doubt upon important aspects of the faith. His letter concluded: "What the layman wants to know is, Does our Church teach the truth, and if it does, why do a number of our bishops, those we were led to believe held the faith in their keeping, dispute it?" The question is a fair one. The answer? One can only reply that the faith of the Church itself is quite clear, and it is the same yesterday, today, and forever.

But changes in thinking, language, and custom, not to mention the increasing body of scientific knowledge, require that the faith be newly interpreted in each generation. Yet divisions within the Church make it impossible for any body today to define the faith for the universal Church as the great Councils did when the Church was undivided. When an individual, even a bishop, with the best will in the world, tries to restate the faith in terms of contemporary knowledge, he may, and often does, sow the tares of confusion along with the good grain of enlightenment.

In 1960 the House of Bishops of the Episcopal Church, in response to a petition from some four thousand laymen, reaffirmed "the Rock of our faith." In a pastoral letter, the Bishops declared:

Anglican Churches are clearly and unequivocally committed to the Apostles' and Nicene Creeds as the symbols of that faith. . . . By continuous Prayer Book worship, by teaching, by preaching, and by our position in all Church unity discussions, the Episcopal Church has shown its loyalty to the historic Creeds.

This position is held because the Creeds are rooted in the biblical record of God's historical acts in Christ. It is the purpose of the Creeds

to preserve the meaning of the historical revelation of God in Christ and
to witness to the revelatory facts in their historicity and givenness. . . .
The Creeds summarize the good news proclaimed by the Primitive
Church, as recorded in the New Testament. The Creeds are a proclama-
tion of a gift, a gift whose kind and nature does not in itself change
from generation to generation. Under the guidance of the Spirit, however, man can grow in appreciation and understanding of this gift . . .

The faith of the Apostolic Church as gathered up in the literature
chosen as the canonical New Testament is the final authority for
Anglicanism. The Creeds are the skeleton of the Bible, and the Bible is
the flesh and blood of the Creeds. The Bible and the Creeds are seen
together, each interpreting the other, with the Bible as the ultimate
norm.

The faith is changeless in its essentials; but it needs to be interpreted to each generation in a language that can be understood
by the people of that age. No one is concerned today with the
medieval argument about how many angels could dance on the
point of a needle; but many are perplexed about how the scientific
world of atoms and molecules fits into traditional Christian thought.
The threat of nuclear destruction of humanity poses problems un-
known to our forefathers and demands a new consideration of the
"last things": death, judgment, heaven, and hell. The problem of an
exploding population, the development of cheap contraceptives, the
so-called "new morality"—all these and a host of current and important subjects require not that the teachings of Christianity be
changed, but that they be re-examined and applied to the overwhelming problems of modern man.

In the attempt to re-examine, to reinterpret, and to restate
Christian truths in modern terms, it is not surprising that some who
teach in the name of Christianity, however sincere, fall into heresy.
Nevertheless, the process of re-presentation must go on, and in due
course the wisdom of the Church, under the guidance of the Holy
Spirit, will separate truth from error, wheat from chaff.

The Archbishop of Canterbury, one of the great theologians of our day, in a small booklet, analyzes some of the ideas "which may seem to be strange, difficult, revolutionary," in the works of some contemporary writers.

As a Church we need to be grappling with the questions and trials of belief in the modern world. Since the war our Church has been too inclined to be concerned with the organizing of its own life, perhaps assuming too easily that the faith may be taken for granted and needs only to be stated and commended. But we state and commend the faith only in so far as we go out and put ourselves with loving sympathy inside the doubts of the doubting, the questions of the questioners, and the loneliness of those who have lost their way.

It is possible for Christians to bear shocks and not to find them wholly destructive. It has been a characteristic of our Anglican portion of the Holy Catholic Church to learn from episodes of human thought without becoming in bondage to them. It was possible to learn from the Darwinian revolution in the last century a greater understanding of the divine process of Creation without becoming dominated by a dogma of automatic progress. It was possible earlier in this century to learn from the rigors of New Testament criticism without submitting to the liberal theory of Harnack or the scepticism of Bultmann. So too some of us have faced the message of a Kierkegaard or a Karl Barth and through the deep darkness have learned more fully of the greatness of God and the nothingness of man, and have emerged not disciples of Barth's system but people who see their old faith in a new depth.

So today it is for us to be ready to find God not within the cosiness of our own piety but within the agony of the world and the meeting of person with person every day. But wherever we find Him, He is still the God who created us in His own image, and sent His Son to be our Saviour and to bring us to the vision of God in heaven.[3]

What, then, can we Christians of the nuclear age believe?

We can believe the faith of our fathers, as set forth in the Bible and the creeds, as taught by our Lord through the holy Catholic Church. No discoveries of the physical or social sciences, no inventions, no reinterpretations can destroy that which is true. The Lord our God is one God, and he is the God of truth. The secrets of the universe, the power of nuclear fission, the macrocosm of the galaxies, and the microcosm of the atoms, are his, and he made them. We need not fear truth from any source, for all truth is of God. Thus today, as in ages past and in ages yet to come, we can confidently stand and say: "I believe in God . . . in Jesus Christ his only Son our Lord . . . in the Holy Ghost: the holy Catholic Church; The Communion of Saints: The Forgiveness of sins: The Resurrection of the body: And the Life everlasting. Amen."

What Is the Church?

CHAPTER TWO

THE word *church* has such a variety of meanings that it is well for us to define the term for the purposes of this book. If you look in a big dictionary, such as *Webster's New International* (2nd ed.), you will find no less than eight definitions of *church*. Not the least interesting is the verb *to church,* appearing in slang usage, as "to church a watch"—thieves' jargon for taking the works out of a stolen watch and leaving only the case to be palmed off on an unsuspecting victim. One hopes that definition is not appropriate to his own parish!

Spelled with a small *c, church* normally refers either to the building in which Christians worship or to the worshiping congregation itself. In New Testament times there were few if any buildings specifically set apart for Christian worship; the local congregation of Christians met in a private home or, in times of persecution, in a cave or catacomb. It was not the place of worship, but the congregation of the faithful, which was important. Thus the letters of the Apostles, which we know as epistles, were addressed to "the church of God that is at Corinth," or to "the churches of Galatia." Each of the local churches was probably at first a single congregation, meeting wherever it could; later the term came to include several congregations in a given city or locality, perhaps with separate ministers but grouped together under one Apostle or a bishop.

There is a second sense in which the word was used in the New Testament, and in which it is still used today. When it is so used, it is generally spelled with a capital *C* and designates the Church universal—that is, the body of all duly baptized Christians, united in one visible fellowship wherever they might be. The Jews thought that the Church of the Old Testament was confined to Israel, a nation. Our Lord showed that it was for *all* nations and, therefore, universal. It is universal (one over-all) because he is one. Many groups do not make it one. The Church is one because he is one and because there is one faith, one baptism, one God and Father of us all. This is the Church which our Lord foreshadowed in such a statement as "I am the vine and ye are the branches" and to which St. Paul applied such powerful metaphors as "bride of Christ" and "Body of Christ." As time went on, the term was applied also to the faithful departed as well as the living so that, in its broadest sense, the word *Church* applies to all who bear or have borne the name of Christians throughout all the eras of history. Moreover, since Christianity is a continuous development from the Jewish religion, there is a sense in which the prophets and people of the Old Testament may be considered as part of the Church universal, even though they did not so regard themselves.

Between the narrowest and broadest definitions of the word *church* are many intermediate ones. We may speak of the Episcopal Church, or the Presbyterian Church, or the Church of Latter Day Saints, or the Church of God, or the Roman Catholic Church. They are descriptive denominational names, and in using the names, we are not necessarily committing ourselves to any specific doctrine or belief about them. We do not mean, for example, that the Episcopal Church is the only one having bishops, or that presbyters are to be found only among Presbyterians, contemporary saints only among Mormons, or followers of God only in the Pentecostal bodies, nor would we concede that catholicity is to be found only within the Roman Catholic Church.

The Book of Common Prayer defines the Church as "the Body of which Jesus Christ is the Head and all baptized people are the members." This definition is fully in accord with the New Testament use of the word; it accords as well with the historic Creeds which describe the Church as "One, Holy, Catholic, and Apostolic."

The Prayer Book further elaborates upon the "notes" of the Church by saying that

> . . . the Church is
>
> One; because it is one Body under one Head;
>
> Holy; because the Holy Spirit dwells in it, and sanctifies its members;
>
> Catholic; because it is universal, holding earnestly the Faith for all time, in all countries, and for all people; and is sent to preach the Gospel to the whole world;
>
> Apostolic; because it continues stedfastly in the Apostles' teaching and fellowship.

As we look about us in the world, or even in our own community, it is difficult for us to identify any visible society or body to which these four notes seem to apply. The Church is obviously not one—unless we adopt the popular Roman Catholic view that only those local churches deriving their authority from the Pope constitute the true Church and that the rest are either impostors or belong to some vague and undefined entity called "the soul of the Church." We look at our own sins and shortcomings, and those of our fellow members, and find it hard to see holiness as a distinctive mark of the Church. If the Church is Catholic or universal, how can we account for so many varieties and contradictions among groups and individuals? Furthermore, in what sense, if any, can we rightly claim to be apostolic?

All Christians, at least those who belong to a communion of the historic Church, would agree that the four notes *ought* to characterize the Church, and most would say that we should work toward a united Church in which those characteristics would be apparent to all men. The notes are included, for example, in the statement adopted by the Assembly of the World Council of Churches in 1961, outlining the kind of unity we all seek; but is it possible to find the four notes fully expressed in any existing church or communion of churches which belongs to the Council?

Perhaps it would be well if each of us would try to look for these notes in his own church or denomination to see how closely it may, or may not, measure up to the ideal. Surely there is a unity that underlies all our divisions—the unity of faith in Jesus Christ, in his revelation of the nature of God the Father, and in the power of the Holy Spirit in the lives of men. That is basic Christianity, for without that essential portion of the faith no man can truly call himself a Christian. So, too, the acceptance of the Holy Scriptures is a bond that unites all Christians, despite various interpretations of the same. Those two things alone set apart the Christian from those who profess any other religion or no religion at all; and they form a powerful bond of unity, one that is stronger than our diversity.

What about holiness? We must remember that the Church has a dual nature. It is a divine organism, the Body of Christ, and as such, it shows forth in all ages and in all places the holiness of its Lord in his divine humanity and human divinity. It is composed, however, of sinful men and women like you and me—men and women and children for whom our Lord died, not because we are worthy, but in order to save us from our sins. The holiness of the Church is the holiness of our Lord. Yet we, too, are holy persons— made holy in Baptism, set apart and hallowed to God's use and praise. Through the recognition of this fact we see holiness both as a state of being and as a process of growth—growing in holiness, or growing away from it but never completely getting outside it. In every age there have been members of the Church who, by their response to his holiness, by their growth in holiness, have risen to what we call sainthood. And these saints were also sinners, for even the greatest sinners have within themselves the potentiality of sainthood. There were saints even in the days of the Church's greatest corruption, because the holiness of its divine nature as the Body of Christ prevailed. And there will be sinners as long as the world endures because man's sinful nature, too, endures.

Catholicity is a note which some people find hard to define, largely because the word *Catholic*—one of the great watchwords of the Church—has become a partisan and sometimes even a fighting word. The Roman Catholics at times have tried to appropriate it exclusively for themselves; and all too many Orthodox, Anglicans, and Protestants seem willing to let them get away with it. Properly speaking, *Catholic* means universal, pertaining to the whole Church; the antithesis is not *Protestant* but *sectarian,* pertaining to only a part of the Church. That Church is truly Catholic which holds earnestly the faith for all time—the full Christian faith, neither adding to it unscriptural dogmas, nor subtracting from it scriptural doctrines. As the Prayer Book definition indicates, true Catholicity involves also a lively sense of mission to the whole world. A Church or an individual is not truly Catholic if it (or he) either tampers with the faith of the universal Church or tries to hold onto it in smug self-satisfaction for himself, his nation, or his own particular group or parish.

What about apostolicity? A Church (or an individual) is apostolic when it (or he) "continues stedfastly in the Apostles' teaching and fellowship." That is, the Church to which he gives his allegiance must be one unbroken continuity with the Church of the New Testament. The book of Acts states that the disciples "continued stedfastly in the Apostles' doctrine and fellowship, in the breaking of bread, and in prayer." The Holy Communion, and the liturgy which contains it, is of the essence of apostolicity. So is the unbroken fellowship of the Apostles, passed down through Christian history by Holy Baptism, with water and the Holy Spirit; and by the hands of the Apostles and their successors, the bishops of the universal Church, in confirmation and ordination.

That last note of the Church is perhaps the most controversial today. Most of the Protestant groups have rejected the episcopate, and in so doing cut themselves off from one of the most important elements of apostolicity. It is not for us who belong to communions that retain the Apostolic Succession to "unchurch" those who have lost it, but rather to continue to hold it in trust for the reunited body of the future, as an indispensable element of "One, Holy, Catholic, Apostolic Church."

Coming back to our definition of the word *church,* we find that it is not a simple one, and that in fact we need a series of graduated definitions. Perhaps we can make this clearer by picturing the relationship of our local parish to the widening circles of the regional, national, and world-wide Christian fellowship.

If our local church is an Episcopal church, it is part of a diocese, presided over by a bishop. The diocese in turn is a part of the Protestant Episcopal Church in the United States, administered by the Presiding Bishop. The Episcopal Church is a part of the Anglican Communion, with the Archbishop of Canterbury as its titular head; and the Anglican Communion is a part of "the One, Holy, Catholic and Apostolic Church" to which we declare our allegiance in the creeds.

Thus the parish church is for us the center of an increasing number of circles that unite us with Christians in every nation of the world; yet even it is not the whole Christian Church. When we recite our belief in the holy Catholic Church, we combine with it the phrase "the Communion of Saints." By that "comfortable doctrine" we mean that the Church as it exists today is one with the Church of the ages, and reaches back in time to the tiny fellowship of our Lord and his Apostles, and has its roots even farther back, in the people of God in the Old Testament times. We mean too that it reaches forward into the future beyond the times of our children and our children's children to ages unborn, even to the end of the life of mankind, and the end of the world.

For all we know, however, even that may not be the full extent of the Church. Our Lord said: "And other sheep I have, which are not of this fold; . . . and there shall be one fold, and one shepherd" (John 10:16). Perhaps in the divine wisdom he had reference to creatures on other planets beyond our solar system, beyond our galaxy, beyond the comprehension of our imagination. Perhaps some day we may find ourselves in communication with some of those "other sheep." If so, let us remember that they, too, are part of God's creation, part of his design.

There are also "angels and archangels and all the company of heaven"—that host of heavenly beings who serve God unceasingly and with whom we proclaim our unity in every celebration of the Holy Communion. It is a great and glorious company, the extent of which no man can number, any more than he can count the grains of sand on all the beaches in the world.

The Church is not something vague and indefinite, nor does it depend upon the changing habits and customs of its members. It is a divine society, given by God and existing both in heaven and on earth. In the words of a contemporary Anglican theologian:

The Church is not the company of the elect, whose names are known only to God. Nor is it a name for the sum of all those "who love the Lord Jesus"; for if it were, it could not be compared by St. Paul to a body. A body is organized; each member has its own function, and all are subject to the head; it also has its definite limits. If the Church is a body, or is at all similar to a body, it must be an organized community; and it cannot be organized unless the names of its members are known. From the apostolic age until to-day, the great majority of Christians have always held that the Church is a visible society. St. Paul and St. John certainly thought so. They knew who was a member, and who was not. . . . Admission was by baptism only; and a member might be deprived of the privileges of his membership. Every local church had its officers: the universal Church also had officers, the Apostles. . . .

The Church is not a contractual society, but an organic society. The members are not prior to the Church; the Church is prior to her members. The bond of union is not contract, but birth; not, indeed, natural birth, but the new birth which is conveyed by baptism. A man cannot join the Church, as he would join a golf club. If he wishes to become a Christian, he must fulfil the conditions of repentance and faith, and pass through a period of instruction and of testing—called the catechumenate—and then be admitted to the Church by baptism. This is the gift of God, and is the first stage in the change of his whole nature. His life begins afresh: he is born again. What he becomes by baptism, he cannot cease to be. He may be a bad Christian, he may be excommunicated, he may betray his religion, but he cannot cease entirely to be a member of the Church, or get rid of the effect of his baptism. . . .

The Church is not, as some have thought, a concession to fallen human nature. She is the environment for which man was created, and in which he is intended to live for ever and ever.[1]

What then shall we say of the relationship between the one Church of the creeds and the welter of churches, denominations, and sects into which Christendom is divided? We cannot equate *The Church* with any of them or with all of them together.

Perhaps, though, a verbal diagram may help us to find at least a partial answer. Suppose we draw a large circle to represent "the One, Holy, Catholic, Apostolic Church." In the center will be a cross, representing belief in Jesus Christ. Surrounding it are the four elements which the Anglican Communion has set forth as essential to a reunited Church: the scriptures, the creeds, the sacraments, and the historic episcopate. Farther out in the circle, we may place symbols representing distinguishing notes of the major communions: mysticism for Eastern Orthodoxy, papal supremacy for Roman Catholics, the Prayer Book for Anglicans, private judgment for Protestants. Still farther out (but still in a large circle) we might place other symbols for less generally accepted doctrines and concepts, to name a few: the Assumption of the Blessed Virgin Mary; compulsory confession; evangelistic revivals, the practice of speaking with tongues.

Now try to draw a line incorporating the things that are taught and practiced in your own Church. It will not be a circle. It will of course include the central cross of Christ. In addition it will include some but not all of the symbols representing other doctrines and practices. It will therefore be distorted, even wavy; and Christ will no longer be at the center of it.

How are we to find the true Church amid so much irregularity and wobbliness? We must start with Christ at the center, and draw the circle large enough to embrace all Christian elements. No doubt some of the symbols will have to be erased, and others modified; but each tradition must contribute its treasures to the whole, without distortion. The universal Church of the creeds is not just the sum of the major communions of Christendom; it is greater than any of them, even greater than all of them combined; it is a perfect circle, with the cross of Christ at the center. The closer we draw to that central cross, the closer we shall come to each other and to the unity of the Church.

One note of caution should be expressed, however: Christian unity will never come about simply by trying to paste existing churches and denominations together, or by rearranging them in such a way that everything—truth and error, essentials and nonessentials—is somehow gathered together to form a superchurch. Important as unity is to the fullness of the Church, truth and holiness are equally important. I cannot express the matter better than by quoting from the magnificent address of Michael Ramsey, Archbishop of Canterbury, to the Third Assembly of the World Council of Churches at New Delhi in 1961.

Pointing out that Christ, our great High Priest, had prayed for unity, holiness, and truth for his followers, the Archbishop said that fulfillment of the prayer is indivisible. He said:

It is useless to think that we can look for unity in Christ's name unless we are looking no less for holiness in his obedience and for the realization of the truth he has revealed.

The World, caring [as it does] for unity, is shocked when the Church fails to manifest it. Yet while the world's criticism must rightly humble us, we must not on that account accept the world's conception of the matter. It is not just unity . . . that we seek . . . it is for unity and truth and holiness that we work and pray. . . . A movement which concentrates on unity as an isolated concept can mislead the world and mislead us, as indeed would a movement which had the exclusive label of holiness or the exclusive label of truth. . . .

"I believe in one Church"; we do not learn to say that. We learn to say, "I believe in one, holy, catholic, apostolic Church," and the notes of the Church are a symphony in depth telling of the depth of Christ's prayer and of the depth of the fulfillment.

The Archbishop is, of course, quite right. The unity of the Church is indeed important; so important that our Lord himself prayed for it in the garden of Gethsemane, in an agony of devotion that brought great drops of blood to his sacred brow. Yet holiness, catholicity, and apostolicity are equally marks of the universal Church, and if true Christian unity is to be achieved no one of the notes must be suppressed in favor of another.

That is why, when we pray for the Church, we ask God

to fill it with all truth, in all peace. Where it is corrupt, purify it; where it is in error, direct it; where in anything it is amiss, reform it. Where it is right, establish it; where it is in want, provide for it; where it is divided, reunite it; for the sake of him who died and rose again, and ever liveth to make intercession for us, Jesus Christ, thy Son, our Lord. *Amen.* (Book of Common Prayer, page 37)

The Role of the Laity

CHAPTER THREE

In spite of the misuse of the word *layman* in contemporary speech—lawyers referring to non-lawyers as laymen, nudists to non-nudists, and so on—the word has a long history of use with religious meaning. It comes from the Greek word *laos,* meaning the body of all faithful people. The word as such does not appear in the New Testament, but three other words adequately describe the layman's task.

The first word is *steward.* "As every man hath received the gift, even so minister the same one to another, as good stewards of the manifold grace of God," says the First Epistle of St. Peter. A steward is one who occupies a position of trust for the administration of something belonging to someone else. The gift of the grace of God in the Christian religion is given to us not for our own special and selfish benefit, but that we may minister it to one another as good stewards. In other words, our religion is not something to keep to ourselves but rather something that we must share with others if we are to be faithful to our vocation as Christian laymen.

The second word is *witness.* "Ye shall also bear witness, because ye have been with me from the beginning," says our Lord. A witness is someone who bears true testimony out of his own experience. The first disciples were witnesses to the Resurrection, their eye-witnessing has been handed down from one generation to another by the faithful. No event in history is so well attested as the Resurrection—and the Resurrection is what makes it possible for us to believe Jesus Christ and to believe in him. Hearsay evidence is rapidly thrown out of any court and a man on the witness stand is required by the judge to speak the truth, the whole truth, and nothing but the truth, out of his own knowledge and experience. Our job as Christian witnesses is to live our lives and exert our influence in accordance with the Christian experience that is ours.

The third word frequently used in the New Testament to describe the layman is *disciple.* A disciple is one who not only learns from another person but also follows him as a personal leader. At Confirmation we are asked: "Do you promise to follow Jesus Christ as your Lord and Saviour?" Each of us replies individually "I do," and so we take upon ourselves the definite responsibility of Christian discipleship.

This is our job as laymen—to follow Christ; and that we do when we worship God every Sunday in his Church, and work and pray and give for the spread of his kingdom. The layman has a special and important share in the building of that kingdom, an opportunity and a task that often he alone can perform.

No bishop, priest, or deacon can present the reality of our religion to worldliness in quite the same way as a layman can. Religion for the clergy and religion for lay people are necessarily different things. To be sure, there is no double standard: at bottom they are subject to the same law and strive for the same end. But a clergyman's religion is closely intertwined with his temporal concerns: his office, his social position, his responsibilities as a pastor, his professional skill. He bears the mark of an order, a caste, and nobody who prizes his ministrations would wish that mark to be less distinct than it is. The layman, on the other hand, lives in two very different spheres, the world and the Church. In the world he has no uniform or badge to distinguish him from the millions who labor with him. If he is to be known as a Christian at all, it must be by the most real signs, by the unmistakable salt of grace in every syllable he utters, by a passionate warmth of love in every act he performs. Those are the arguments against which there is no answer. The only resistance they meet comes from the people who would continue unmoved "though one rose from the dead."

Outside our churches the crowds drift by, ailing souls of all degrees: the self-sufficient, the baffled, the ignorant, the oppressed, the defiled. Inside the means of grace are dispensed to an uninspired, inactive few. The crowds would find gratification for every good desire, abundance for every need, if we could gather them within the walls. They run from a priest, they stampede in panic at the sight of a bishop. Who can bring them in? Lay Christians. And how? By being Christians. You are no Christian until you have captured your man.[1]

One of the great ecumenical leaders, Klaus von Bismarck, began his discussion of the laity at the Assembly of the World Council of Churches in 1961 with the statement:

Three weeks ago my wife and I had a conversation with a German missionary from South Africa. We asked him: "How do you preach to your people?" He gave us one example:

The kraal of our Zulus is a hedge of thorns, a protection from danger. One day a calf that didn't know any better wanted to get out because it smelled the fresh grass outside. The calf gradually pushed its way through the protective thicket and got out. Its mother followed it and, eventually, so did the whole herd. The herd scattered and, thus, unprotected, soon fell prey, one by one to the wild animals.

"The space that the thorn hedge so wisely protects is the Church, the place of the Christian congregation. Therefore," reasoned the African missionary, "stay in the kraal, in the place protected by the Church. Don't be tempted, particularly when you are young, by the apparently greener pastures outside. But if you stay together within the family circle of the congregation, you will be safe in God's keeping."

The "kraal concept" of the laity, observed Dr. von Bismarck, is one that seems to appeal to certain theologians but is in itself quite inadequate. The role of the laity is far more important than that of a domestic animal!

Unfortunately, though many laymen do think of themselves as merely passive members of the Church or as the ultimate beneficiaries of the ministrations of the clergy, nothing could be further from the true concept of the layman's role in the Church.

Much is said in contemporary church assemblies of "the ministry of the laity," and even of "the theology of the laity," terms which are often confusing to laymen who hear them for the first time. Occasionally they seem to be merely a part of the theological jargon used by the clergy. The second of the terms, "the theology of the laity," is especially confusing. I do not like it because it assumes that there are two theologies, one for the clergy and another for the laity, and that is absurd: the faith of the Church is one and applies equally to all persons, clerical or lay, in every age and nation. Theology is essentially man's knowledge of God, and it cannot be different for different classes, races, nations, or denominations of Christians.

The term "the ministry of the laity" or, as sometimes given, "the priesthood of all believers" may also be confusing at first sight, but it represents something that is true and essential in the life of the Church.

We become Christians at Baptism. At that time we make certain promises, or certain promises are made for us by our sponsors: we renounce, in the words of the Prayer Book, "the devil and all his works, the vain pomp and glory of the world, with all covetous desires of the same, and the sinful desires of the flesh." We affirm belief in "all the Articles of the Christian Faith, as contained in the Apostles' Creed." We express our desire to be baptized in that faith and promise that we will "obediently keep God's holy will and commandments, and walk in the same all the days of [our] life."

By making those promises, we receive certain benefits. They are set forth in the fourfold prayer of the ministry of Baptism, to each portion of which the congregation assents with the word *Amen*.

O merciful God, grant that like as Christ died and rose again, so *this child* . . . may die to sin and rise to newness of life. *Amen*.

Grant that all sinful affections may die in *him,* and that all things belonging to the Spirit may live and grow in *him. Amen*.

Grant that *he* may have power and strength to have victory, and to triumph, against the devil, the world, and the flesh. *Amen*.

Grant that whosoever is here dedicated to thee by our office and ministry, may also be endued with heavenly virtues, and everlastingly rewarded, through thy mercy, O blessed Lord God, who does live, and govern all things, world without end. *Amen*.

In Baptism we share in God's mighty act of redemption. We "die to sin and rise to newness of life," as our Lord died for our sins and rose again to assure us of eternal life. Through baptism by water, and in the name of the Trinity, and the signing of the cross upon our forehead, we accept our share in the eternal sacrifice of Christ and are dedicated to be his faithful soldier and servant to our life's end.

Baptism is the sacrament of our initiation into the family of God. In the early Church, and in Eastern Orthodox churches today, Baptism was immediately followed by Confirmation as the completion of the rite of initiation. In our western Church, Confirmation has been deferred to the "years of discretion" in order that the Christian may reaffirm the promises made for him when he was baptized; but essentially Baptism and Confirmation, whether administered at the same time or separated in time, constitute the rite of Christian initiation.

The true Confirmation prayer is that of the bishop just before he lays his hand upon the head of each candidate:

Almighty and everliving God, who has vouchsafed to regenerate these thy servants by Water and the Holy Ghost, and hast given unto them forgiveness of all their sins; Strengthen them, we beseech thee, O Lord, with the Holy Ghost, the Comforter, and daily increase in them thy manifold gifts of grace: the spirit of wisdom and understanding, the spirit of counsel and ghostly strength, the spirit of knowledge and true godliness; and fill them, O Lord, with the spirit of thy holy fear, now and for ever. *Amen.*

St. Paul defines the laity as "fellow citizens with the saints and of the household of God" (Ephesians 2:19), and adds "for through Christ ye are no more strangers and foreigners but fellow citizens with the saints . . . In whom all the building fitly framed together groweth unto an holy temple in the Lord: In whom ye also are builded together for an habitation of God through the Spirit."

Thus the baptized and confirmed person takes his place as a

layman in the life of the Church with the same seriousness as a bishop or priest, and all share in the reconciliation of the world to Christ and in the spread of his kingdom to all peoples.

There is, of course, an important difference between the functions of the clergy and those of the laity. Bishops, priests, and deacons have the special functions of administering the sacramental life of the Church, of preaching and teaching, and of ministering to the congregations; they alone are the guardians of the sacraments of the Church and of its faith and order. But in the world the layman has his distinct and essential ministry as a fully accredited and commissioned and, in a sense, ordained ambassador of Christ. Those in Holy Orders conduct their business at the altar and in the pulpit; the layman conducts his business in society.

We confuse the matter when we speak of a man who is to be ordained as "going into the Church"; we laymen are just as much in the Church, by virtue of our Baptism and Confirmation, as is a priest or bishop, or even the Archbishop of Canterbury. We are not meant to be a part of the problems which the Church faces, but a part of the solution. The problems of the Church are also our problems, and the task of reconciliation is also our task.

We *laymen* are the Church. Along with the clergy we form the *laos*—the people of God in this generation, and as such, we are heirs of the assignment given by our Lord to all of his people, to go into the world and make disciples of all nations.

In another analogy, not so popular today as in the past, we are the army of the Lord. The bishops may be the generals and the priests the officers of the army; but we laymen form the rank and file. It is our task to storm the breastworks of the enemy and to win the day for our Lord and his Church.

It is in fact the laity who have been in the vanguard in every great age in which the Church made notable advances. St. Paul's missionary journey, as extensive as it was, covered only a portion of the Roman Empire, the civilized world of his day. It was little groups of laymen centered about the local bishop in scores of communities who kept the faith alive during the first three centuries of the Church's life. When the Church emerged from persecution, it was mostly the laymen, including soldiers of the empire, who carried Christianity to the far corners of the earth. Without the devotion, the prayers, and the sacrifices of lay people, Christianity would soon have become a mystical philosophy of the few instead of the dynamic religion of the many.

Laymen are the channel of communication between the Church and the world. Our task is not so much to promote the faith by talking about it (although that is a part of our duty), but to show forth Christianity by living it.

The Book of Common Prayer sums up the function of the laity in a Collect that should be familiar to every Churchman:

Direct us, O Lord, in all our doings, with thy most gracious favour, and further us with thy continual help; that in all our works begun, continued, and ended in thee, we may glorify thy holy Name, and finally, by thy mercy, obtain everlasting life; through Jesus Christ our Lord. *Amen.*

Bishops and Priests

CHAPTER FOUR

WE HAVE talked so much about the role of the laity in the preceding chapter that we may be accused of belittling the clergy and thinking of Christianity as exclusively a lay religion. Nothing could be further from our intention.

The sacred ministry is the highest vocation to which a man may be called. It is the ministry of reconciliation, and the care of the faithful, the forgiveness of the sinner, the comforting of the sick and sorrowful, the commendation of the dying. It is placed at the vital point where God and man meet. It is the assumption, at God's command and with his authority, of the awesome responsibility for the health and welfare of human souls. It is the solemn responsibility for the preaching of the Word and for the ministration of the Church's sacraments.

The sacred ministry is at once a great privilege and a weighty obligation. It brings overwhelming joy and profound sadness. It is a vocation of which no man feels himself worthy but to which he devotes his life, his self, his all. God be praised for the thousands, and hundreds of thousands, of devoted servants of Christ who exercise the sacred ministry in all lands, in all ages, and among all sorts and conditions of men, women, and children. Parenthetically, let it be said that if the priest has a pastoral concern for his people, the people ought also to have a deep pastoral concern for their priests. The prayers of the laity, their sympathetic understanding, and their willingness to respond, to forgive, are the intangible but powerful reactions that, together with the grace of God, make it possible for a priest to carry out his ministry with the inner serenity and strength that are the marks of a good pastor.

Since this book is written by a layman and primarily for laymen, I would call upon each reader to do all in his power to support the clergy in their enormous task. Let no opportunity pass to speak well of them to others. If you must complain to your priest, do so as kindly and constructively as possible. Do not gossip about him or speak ill of him to others. Uphold his hands in the parish and the community. Above all, pray for him that he may effectively do God's will in the particular ministry to which he has been called. Do not hold a grudge against him, and accept the sacraments from him gladly whatever his faults.

Remember also your bishop, who has not only the responsibility of other ministers but also "the care of all the churches."

"The office of Bishop," in the words of the Offices of Instruction, "is to be chief pastor in the Church; to confer Orders; and to administer Confirmation." He is also to be the Father in God of his clergy and all his people, to teach the faith, and to express the conscience of the Church before the world.

Unfortunately, we have allowed our bishops to become administrators, office workers, money raisers, social adornments, and many other things that are not inherent in the office of a bishop of the Church of God.

My father was a Church publisher and bookseller. When one of his friends was elected to the episcopate, he would write him a letter of congratulation and add, "We are closing your book account as we know you will have no further time either to read or to write books." The statement was, of course, a facetious one but, alas, it contained more than a grain of truth.

The Episcopal Church probably has a higher ratio of bishops to communicants than any other of the historic churches, and one would think, therefore, that our bishops would have a greater amount of time for writing and teaching, for intensified pastoral ministrations, for conducting retreats for the clergy and laity, and, in general, for the important spiritual side of their work. That, however, is not the case. Many of our bishops spend far too much time at their desks and not enough in their oratories; they are to be found more often in airplanes and motorcars than in their studies; and when they visit a parish for Confirmation, they are hurried and harried and entertained to the extent that they rarely have time to discuss the pastoral problems of the parish with their clergy and with the wardens and vestrymen.

In God's name—I say it reverently—isn't it possible for this Church of ours to relieve its bishops of the innumerable secular responsibilities laid upon them so that they can devote more time to their primary calling to be the teachers and chief shepherds of the souls committed to their care?

To a great extent, the same failings can be found in the current practice of the priesthood, particularly among the rectors of parishes, especially the large parishes. The Anglican clergy used to be known as *stupor mundi*—the wonder of the world—because of their carefully prepared preaching and their sound and pastoral scholarship. Today, one rarely finds the name of a priest (or bishop) of the Episcopal Church in a list of best preachers; too often their sermons are either so remote from the needs of the congregation or so concerned with things temporal that they fail to present the scriptural and eternal truths of the faith.

"The Office of a Priest is, to minister to the people committed to his care; to preach the Word of God; to baptize; to celebrate the Holy Communion; and to pronounce Absolution and Blessing in God's Name," and "the office of a Deacon is, to assist the Priest in Divine Service, and in his other ministrations, under the direction of the Bishop."

The priest is a man set apart and ordained for full-time ministry in the Church of God. Ordination gives him a certain "indelible character"—that is, he always remains a priest, whether he proves to be a good one or a bad one. Even if he is deposed for grave cause in accordance with the canons of the Church, or if he voluntarily renounces the ministry, he remains one who has been called to the special work of the care of souls, and of prayer and intercession for

others. That is why some priests, who find after some years in the
ordained ministry that they are not fitted by temperament for the
very exacting work of the parish ministry, nevertheless devote their
lives to some form of religious or social service, or of teaching or
writing. Having once taken up the yoke of the priesthood, they find
that they cannot be entirely relieved of it.

The life of a priest is not an easy one, nor is it intended to be so.
It was not easy for the Apostles, who turned from the normal work-
a-day tasks of fisherman, tax gatherer, or shepherd to become fishers
of men, gatherers of the treasures of human souls, and shepherds of
the wayward flock of Christ. The priest must always renounce the
easy ways of the world, the path of worldly conformity, and the
road to earthly reward. Yet if, in the slow progress of the building of
the kingdom of God, the way of the priesthood demands sacrifice
and involves disappointment and mental anguish, as it often does, it
also carries rich rewards of eternal satisfaction and rejoicing.

We laymen rightly expect great things of our parish priest; but
sometimes we expect the wrong things. We tend to judge him by
the standards of worldly success at the same time that we expect him
to renounce the pattern of worldliness. We may forget that he is a
man with the same human interests, the same family responsibilities,
the same need for balancing a budget and for educating his family
that the rest of us have. We may expect him to soar with the wings
of an eagle while subsisting on the bread crumbs set out for spar-
rows. We demand that he give us his time and his best efforts when
we need him, but we may forget that he also has his own problems,
his times of loneliness, and his hours of need when our prayers and
our practical help can be of invaluable assistance to him. Rather
than subject the rector, his wife, and his family to criticism and
gossip, or expect them to be the unpaid servants of the parish, or to
live beyond the means with which we provide them, let us respect
them as our partners in the work of salvation.

The rector of a parish is a man called by God and ordained by
the Church to guide the spiritual lives of those committed to his care

in the community into which he is sent. He is not the employee of
the vestry, nor a hired symbol of respectability. His chief functions
are not to preside at fashionable weddings, to be part of the decor at
christenings, to be a "wheel" in the local service club, or to lend an air
of sanctity at the burial of those who have seldom darkened the door
of the church. He is not called to preach sermons that make us feel
comfortable and self-satisfied or that enhance the acceptable "image"
of the Episcopal Church.

What, then, can we laymen properly expect of the priest who is
the rector of our parish and the shepherd of its congregation?

First, and most important, we can expect him to be a man of
God, a man sent by God, ordained by God, to minister God's word
and sacraments—a man to do God's will and in God's name. Just as
Jesus Christ is the Head of the Church, so the rector (or vicar or
priest-in-charge) is the head of the particular congregation of the
Church over which he presides. He represents among us the Lord of
the Church; he intercedes for us on earth as our Lord intercedes for
us in heaven. We can expect him to be, first and foremost, the
minister of God seven days a week, in or out of the parish, and to
be such not merely when he is performing the specific functions of
the priesthood. This is true of all priests, not just those who are
rectors of parishes.

Second, closely related to, and indeed flowing from, his nature
as a man of God, we can expect him to be a man of prayer. To be
sure, every Christian should be a praying one; but the priest is
called to a life of prayer not only in the public worship of the
Church but in the privacy of his oratory or his study—prayer for the
whole state of Christ's Church and specifically for those among
whom he ministers. We should never hesitate to ask him for his
prayers for any special needs that we may have; and at the same
time, we should not forget to pray for him and his needs. Of course,
we expect him to pray the daily Offices of Morning and Evening
Prayer, either publicly or privately.

We can expect our priest to teach the faith in season and out, the hard facts of the Christian faith as well as the consoling ones. The hardest fact of the Christian life is sin, particularly our own sins. We must expect him, in his teaching, in his preaching, and in his personal ministrations to remind us that we are sinners and also that our Lord, who died for our sins, has shown us the way of contrition, confession, forgiveness, and amendment of life.

We can expect our priest to preach the Word of God, rooted in Holy Scripture and applied to the circumstances of our own time. Not every priest can be an eloquent preacher, nor should we expect him to give a learned dissertation on economics, sociology, or current events, but we can and should expect him to preach the pure doctrine of the scriptures, in accordance with the recurring round of the Christian Year, and with special application to the circumstances of the community, the nation, and the world.

We can expect our priest to devote some part of each day to study and meditation, so that his mind and his soul may be refreshed and the well-springs of his faith replenished. At those times he should never be interrupted, except for serious cause; he cannot be expected always to "give out" without periods of deep drinking in of the Bible and religious books and periodicals. Similarly, we should allow him times of retreat and spiritual refreshment as well as of physical rest and recreation.

We can expect our priest to be with us when we are going through deep waters, in sickness or accident, in trial or perplexity, in personal or family problems. We should not expect him, by some sixth sense, to guess when we really need him for such priestly help; we should telephone or call upon him or somehow get word to him that we are in need of help; and the good priest will never fail us.

We can also invite the priest to share with us in times of rejoicing and gladness, and to give thanks for us and with us at God's manifold blessings upon ourselves, our households, our loved ones. Too often the priest is called upon for help only in crises, and not for joy and blessings. Like Christ at the marriage in Cana, the priest should be called upon to share the moments of joy in the life of the Christian as well as those of sorrow. After all, he, too, is a member of the household of God.

When we know that we have sinned and that "the burden of our sins is intolerable," we can go to the priest for confession and for spiritual guidance. There is nothing peculiar or "high Church" about the sacrament of Penance; it is a normal part of the Church's life. We can expect the priest to set apart regular times for confession, to announce them as such, and not to disguise them as "office hours" or by some such phrase as "the rector will be in Church on Saturdays from 5 to 6." Private confession is not compulsory in the Episcopal Church, but it should be readily available to those who feel the need of it either regularly or in some time of special crisis. Every priest (and bishop) of the Church should be prepared to exercise willingly that portion of his ministry. He was ordained—that is, ordered—to forgive sins.

We can expect the priest to offer the public services of the Church, more especially Holy Communion, regularly, frequently, and at hours convenient to the parish. Moreover, we should avail ourselves of those services not only by meeting the minimal requirement "to worship God every Sunday in his Church" but on or near birthdays and marriage anniversaries, on saints' days, and at other times of special meaning or special need for us.

Are we setting too high a standard for our clergy? Are we setting up the priest as a superman or something other than a normal, friendly human being? I think not. We do not expect our clergy to be plastic saints on a pedestal or to be removed from the normal life of their parishioners; quite the contrary, there is nothing that repels men so much as a priest (or bishop) who is unctuous or "holier than thou," who speaks or preaches with an affected "clerical" voice, or who holds himself aloof from his parishioners and from the community.

If the priest is to be a man of God (and that is his calling), we want him to act like a priest, to dress like a priest (except when he is on vacation, or engaged in sports or physical work) and at all times to be a priest.

A word about forms of address. Personally, I like the title "Father," because it recognizes the priest's position in God's family, the Church. Lutherans and others use the title "Pastor," which conveys much the same meaning. But if a priest prefers to be addressed as "Mister" or "Doctor," if he is so entitled, his wish should be respected. I don't even object to calling a priest "Joe" (if that's his name) on private occasions, or "Father Joe" on public ones. Indeed, it should not be inappropriate for Christians to call each other by their Christian names. The best rule for a layman is to find out how a priest prefers to be addressed and to conform to his preference.

However you address your parish priest or any other priest, or however well you know him, remember first and foremost that he is a man of God. I beseech my fellow laymen to unshackle their priests from a constant round of cocktail parties, civic affairs, parish bazaars, and the routine of the every member canvass, so that they may more effectively carry out the job for which they were ordained. *Let the priest be a priest.* Let him have time to study, to prepare his sermons and, above all, to pray—at least to say his daily Offices. Give him the opportunity of rejoicing with his flock at the times of rejoicing, and of strengthening the sick, the sorrowful, and those who are in need; of counseling and absolving the sinners (including ourselves), and of carrying out the office and work of a priest in the Church of God. Count him as a member of the household of the faithful, not a public relations officer.

If you need help, go to him at the altar or in the confessional, or for spiritual counsel to his study. If, for any reason, you need him, feel free to call upon him; don't sit back and complain because he doesn't call on you as often as you think he should. Remember he is nobody's private chaplain. He probably has others who need his services more than you do, and when you are in need, he will be only too happy to respond to your call.

Let me add here a word in appreciation of the members of religious orders—monks and nuns—in the Episcopal Church. They are little known to many Episcopalians, and less appreciated; though it is said that there are today more members of religious orders in the Anglican churches than there were when Henry VIII dissolved the monasteries and convents. They are men and women who have renounced much that the world holds dear—the hope of wealth, marriage and family life, and the freedom to determine their own activities—for love of God and his Church. If Christians are the salt of the world, the members of religious orders are the spice of the Christian Church. They hold constantly before us, in the complete dedication of their lives to God, the goal that should be the aim of every Christian. Remember them in your prayers.

Remember, too, your rector, the other clergy of your parish, the bishop of your diocese, and all the bishops, priests, and deacons of the Church.

Almighty God, the giver of all good gifts, who of thy divine providence hast appointed divers Orders in thy Church; Give thy grace, we humbly beseech thee, to all those who are called to any office and administration in the same; and so replenish them with the truth of thy doctrine, and endue them with innocency of life, that they may faithfully serve before thee, to the glory of thy great Name, and the benefit of thy holy Church; through Jesus Christ our Lord. *Amen.*

(Book of Common Prayer, page 39)

The World Is My Parish

IF THE title of this chapter sounds presumptuous, I must protest that it is not mine but a quotation from John Wesley. Because the Church in the eighteenth century rejected his message, we lost the Methodists from our fellowship. Today they number more than eight million in the United States to our three and a half million members.

We lost more than that: because of the complacency of the Church we lost (for a time) the world view of "One, Holy, Catholic, Apostolic Church"—the People of God. The eighteenth century Evangelical Movement awakened the Church from its complacency, and the nineteenth century Oxford Movement renewed our concept of the Catholicity of the Church. Today we are beginning to regain the world view of the Church as the People of God, to think in world terms, and the opportunity to make up for two hundred years of lost time is here. We are, however, still hindered by narrow parochialism and lack of vision; and "without vision, the people perish."

If we would not perish we must enlarge our concept of parish. The word *parish* is defined in my dictionary as "a portion or subdivision of a diocese committed to the spiritual jurisdiction or care of a priest or minister, called *rector* or *pastor*. In the Protestant Episcopal Church, it is a territorial division usually following civil bounds, as those of a town."

In the early Christian Church each area was administered by a bishop and his attendant presbyters and deacons, and was frequently called *parochia*. As the Church grew, it was impossible for the bishop to be physically present in every house of worship, and gradually his diocese was divided into many parishes, each with a priest at its head. The duty of the priest was as it is now: to administer the holy sacraments, to preach the word of God, and to lead the worship of the faithful. In old English terminology, he was known as the *parson*—another way of saying "person." He was essentially "the person" of the community, the one who in the eyes of God and of the state represented the *person* of Christ to all of the Christian souls who made up that particular community.

In other words, the parish was not simply a group of like-minded individuals attending church in a specified place, but it was a portion of the Church universal. It was a whole community on its knees in worship of almighty God. That is still the ideal concept of the parish, but in our divided pluralistic society it has become sadly narrowed in the eyes of most people, even of those who make up the faithful core of church membership.

Recently a rector of a New York parish made newspaper headlines by his exposure of slum conditions, graft, and bribery in the tenements of his parish. It was not for the "faithful worshipers" in his parish that he went to bat, but for the *people* who lived in that area. He recognized them all—black or white, American or foreign, good or bad—as children of God and as part of his responsibility as the pastor to that area. Wasn't that the normal thing for him to do? According to our definition of a parish, it certainly was; yet it was so unusual that it became the subject of newspaper stories and telecasts. The normal was the unusual.

Someone has said that God is not only, nor even primarily, interested in religion. By that I suppose he meant that what goes on in our churches is not so important as what goes on in the world. If, however, the parish is one and the same thing as the community, we get quite a different picture. What goes on across the tracks from the parish church or in the next block is, indeed, a parish concern.

Please don't misunderstand me. I don't mean that the parish should try to be a law enforcement agency, or that the rector, wardens, and vestrymen should constitute themselves a watch-and-ward society. We had an unhappy example of that sort of thing when certain church groups—not Episcopalians, primarily—helped afflict this country with Prohibition. The result of that noble experiment was the establishment of a criminal society which exists to this day. According to *Life* magazine (September 9, 1957) 10 cents out of every dollar spent in the United States goes to crime. We continue to have examples of attempts in the name of religion to suppress books, to censor movies, and to deny birth control information to those who request it. The attempt of any religious body to force its doctrines upon those outside its fold is different from the infamous Spanish Inquisition only in degree, not in kind.

The Church, of course, does stand for righteousness and for justice and mercy to all men, and whatever concerns the community should be of concern to the parish church of that community. Our Lord said, "Except your righteousness shall exceed the righteousness of the scribes and Pharisees [the faithful worshipers of the time] ye shall in no case enter into the kingdom of heaven" (Matt. 5:20).

Ernest Southcott puts it this way:

The Church is to bring the completeness, the wholeness of Christ to the whole man. Each person as a member of the community is to "grow unto the measure of the stature of the fullness of Christ." Sin and disease prevent Christ's wholeness. So the Church is to minister to the sick in mind, body, and spirit, and thus, in a wonderful way to complete Christ. Thus the Church is a redeemed and a redeeming community, carrying on Christ's atoning work for the whole of creation. There is a Zulu saying, "If there is a thorn in the foot, the whole body must stoop down and take it out." Wherever there is incompleteness, disease, ill health, mistrust, misunderstanding, untruth, there at that point the Church is called to bring Christ's wholeness, His fullness.[1]

The matter of sickness and disease is one of the great concerns of the Church. In our Lord's own ministry, as well as in the primitive Church, healing of body and mind went hand in hand with the healing of the soul. Surely our Lord intended it to be that way, for he promised his followers that they should do even greater works of healing than he had done. In one way that has been so. The science of medicine, which is indebted greatly to Christian teaching and inspiration, today performs miracles of healing that would have been incomprehensible in our Lord's day, or even just a generation ago. Thank God for the modern physician, who is as truly a priest of the body as the minister is a priest of the soul!

Through the ages the Church almost lost the gift of charismatic or spiritual healing. The sacrament of Holy Unction fell into abeyance after Christianity emerged from its early underground existence, only to be revived in the Middle Ages as little more than a preparation for death. In the Reformation, even that survival was lost to separated Christianity, and the Church was generally content to leave healing to the medical profession or to regard sickness as the will of God. In time, because of the Church's neglect of such an important part of its ministry, healing sects arose. Some of them were founded on the denial of suffering which is, in effect, to deny the reality of the Cross, for it is an essential part of Christianity that our Lord suffered and died upon the cross for us men and for our salvation. His suffering was a part of his humanity; if Christ's suffering was real, then our own suffering is real, too, and cannot be dismissed as an invention of our imagination or an error in our thinking.

Thank God the Church is reawakening to the recognition of its ministry of healing! Science pointed the way with its recognition of the close interrelationship of body and mind, and religion gradually recovered the sense that the soul is similarly interrelated to the body and the mind. Here and there priests and physicians began to work together, combining spiritual with physical therapy. In the Prayer Book, the sacrament of Holy Unction or Laying on of Hands was restored not as a preparation for death but as an aid to the restoration of life and health:

I anoint thee with oil (*or* I lay my hand upon thee), in the Name of the Father, and of the Son, and of the Holy Ghost; beseeching the mercy of our Lord Jesus Christ, that all thy pain and sickness of body being put to flight, the blessing of health may be restored unto thee. Amen.

Spiritual healing, as the Church understands it, is not a substitute for medical care but a complement to it; nor is it the special prerogative of a "faith healer," although there are individuals who seem to have a special gift of healing. The prayers of the faithful and the ministrations of the priest are a part of the spiritual arsenal of every parish; and more and more parishes are beginning to make use of them and to find that they are powerful aids to the ministrations of the physician. All healing is of God; neither the priest nor the physician can do more than to apply God's gifts and to bring his laws to bear upon the patient's condition; the rest is up to him.

Closely related to the ministry of healing is the ministry of penitence; indeed, often the one is dependent upon the other. Fortunately, the ministry of penitence has never fallen into abeyance in the Church; indeed, the Church would not be the Church without it. There is no service or rite in the Book of Common Prayer that does not include, in some form or other, the confession of sins and the declaration or prayer of forgiveness. As the fact of sin is universal, the need for penitence and forgiveness is universal, and that also is part of the life of the parish as it is of the individual Christian.

Increasingly, too, the Church is making regular provision for the sacrament of Penance—the personal confession of sin in the presence of the priest, the expression of penitence, the profession of sincere desire for amendment of life, and the authoritative assurance of God's forgiveness and absolution. The Episcopal Church does not require individual confession as does the Roman Catholic Church, but every parish should provide opportunity for it as well as frequent instruction about its availability and value for the health of the soul.

Confession is the most difficult of the Christian sacraments. I have found it so in my own life, and though I was trained in its use, quite properly, at the time of my Confirmation, I have neglected it for long periods of time. I do not like to go to my own parish priest for confession, though he is the normal minister of the sacrament, because I know him too well. I find it difficult to divide my inner spiritual life from my social contacts with him, even though I know that as a priest of God he will regard the seal of the confessional as inviolate. That is a human weakness on my part; the Church, however, recognizes such weakness and permits its children to go to another priest for confession if they prefer to do so. I go to a priest with whom I am not intimately acquainted, and from him I obtain the joyous assurance of God's forgiveness, as refreshing to the soul as is a hot shower to the body after a day of toil and soil.

There is another reason for choosing one's confessor with great care. The sacrament of Penance is more than an occasion for the assurance of forgiveness of sin and of God's love for the sinner. It is also an opportunity for spiritual direction, for guidance in the facing of one's particular spiritual problems, and for the growth of the soul. Therefore the choice of a wise and experienced pastor of souls is of the utmost importance. Wisdom and skill in spiritual direction are not an automatic gift of ordination but are the special endowment (or attribute) of experienced priests who burn with the love of souls and who have the ability to put themselves in the place of the penitent, thus helping him bear his own particular burdens and leading him a step further along the path of spiritual growth. Members of religious orders, who spend much time in prayer and meditation, often have the gift; so do some bishops, some chaplains, and some parish priests, even some curates.

If you have never experienced the joy of forgiveness in the sacrament of Penance, I strongly urge you to seek instruction and then to make your first confession. The best way is to attend a retreat or quiet day, and after much prayer and meditation to ask the retreat conductor to hear your confession and to give you some direction for the growth of your inner life.

In any case, choose your confessor with care. Be sure, if you can, that the priest is one who makes his own confession regularly and who has experience in the cure of souls. Then open your heart to him, confess your sins freely and without reserve, and ask him for his guidance and blessing; "after which" in the words of the Prayer

Book (p. 313), "on evidence of [the penitent's] repentance, the Minister shall assure him of God's mercy and forgiveness."

"Go in peace, your sins are forgiven you"—with those words the whole burden of sin will drop from your shoulders, and you will go forth determined to serve and please him in newness of life, to the honor and glory of his name. There is no joy for the Christian quite like that, believe me.

The inner life of the parish itself, like that of the individual, is important. For that reason, let us forget for the moment about the parish bazaar, the men's club, and other activities of the parish house, and look at the worship that is available in your parish and in mine.

You may be unhappy about the manner in which your parish does certain things: possibly the hours of service are not the most convenient for you; perhaps you would prefer to have the Holy Eucharist instead of Morning Prayer at 11 o'clock, or vice versa; perhaps you do not like the priest's sermons or the vestments he wears, or some peculiarity of his speech or habits; maybe the whole setup of the parish is too high Church or too low Church—if you know what those words really mean. (The fact that they mean different things to different people makes those terms meaningless.) The truth is that virtually every parish church contains more spiritual treasures new and old than you and I have the spiritual ability to use!

For one thing, the church itself is there—at a busy intersection, perhaps, in the heart of a bustling city; in a quiet residential area where children pass it on their way to school or housewives, busy with their shopping, hurry by; or it may be at a rural crossroads surrounded by fields of grain, by country estates, or modest homes of commuters.

Wherever the church is, whether it be large or small, it is a place that is dedicated, consecrated, set apart from the hustle and bustle of daily life. It is open to all, a place of prayer for all the people; an oasis into which one may drop for a refreshing moment or an hour of prayer, of meditation, or just to sit and think in quiet, surrounded by the beauty of holiness. Especially, is it true if the blessed Sacrament be reserved, the flickering light betokening the presence of the Word made flesh, the God made man, who was born, suffered, and died for us men and for our salvation. I have never understood why our Lord's holy presence has sometimes become a matter of controversy, or why so many bishops and priests seem to be afraid of it. Surely there is no danger in the Episcopal Church of too much devotion! Our besetting sin is rather too little devotion to our Lord, especially in his sacramental presence. It is true that God is everywhere, but is it not well to know of a special place in which the troubled soul can find God in a very personal and devotional way? A way in which we can quite literally lay our problems and our doubts before him and go away rested, refreshed, and relieved of the burden that truly can be intolerable? Is it not a purpose of the Church to answer that need?

It was not in splendid services but in quiet prayer and meditation before the blessed Sacrament that Evelyn Underhill, one of the greatest of Anglican mystics, came to know God. Her biographer, Margaret Cropper, relates that often Evelyn Underhill would push open the doors of churches, large or small, and spend an hour of rest and quiet, sometimes not even praying but simply letting God speak to her in what she described as "this place where invocation of the invisible never ceased," and which "had an existence in Eternity not granted to the hurrying city streets."

There is, of course, the regular Sunday service—not always an inspiring experience, sometimes appearing to be, as a skeptic once observed, merely "the reading of the minutes of the last meeting." The choir may have one of its off-days, the youthful server may be inept and distracting, the sermon may be painfully dull. It may well have been on such a Sunday that Theodore Wedel had his first experience of the Episcopal Church, yet for him it was "cataclysmic," bringing him a realization that the Church was something far more than a sect. This is how he describes it:

It was not easy for me at first to understand and appreciate the difference, since the little flock of Episcopalians in our Kansas town was, of course, far from being the local habitation of a national, let alone a state, Church. . . . Yet worship according to the Book of Common Prayer simply *was* the "Church" in a new and horizon-widening form. It was—and this can be the liberating appeal of Anglicanism's Catholic heritage to all fellow Christians who are still confined within sectarian walls of separation—the Church in time as well as in space or merely in the form of a contemporary gathering of believers. The worshipping membership was, somehow, not limited to the gathered flock. Here was the Communion of Saints of the ages at prayer. The prayers were themselves the "common" prayer of uncounted Christians of the past, now mysteriously joining with us in worship though removed from our sight to the Church Triumphant. The little Episcopal chapel, with its struggling flock and underpaid minister, did not count very significantly in the community. It was vastly overshadowed by the rival church structures and congregations next door. But—and this is once more the paradox of the Catholic heritage—I had the strangely moving feeling that a majority was nevertheless in our humble sanctuary.[2]

The author of those words, describing the way in which that simple service in a tiny Kansas church opened his eyes, became the warden of our College of Preachers in Washington and one of the truly great priests of the Church.

The words of the Book of Common Prayer are a treasury of devotion that no Christian has ever been able to exhaust. The collects and other prayers are pure gems of worship that have come out of the spiritual experience of all ages. Let us look at the origin of just one of them.

In the days of the dying empire, the city of Rome was heavily besieged and frequently sacked by the barbarians of the North—the ancestors of many of us, incidentally. No man's life was safe, no one knew what the next day would bring. When the dark night closed down, every man securely barred his doors and windows, fearful that before morning the door might be broken down by the enemy or the house set to the torch. From those days came the little collect that is set in Evening Prayer: "Lighten our darkness, we beseech thee, O Lord; and by thy great mercy defend us from all perils and dangers of this night; for the love of thy only Son, our Saviour, Jesus Christ."

I have used this prayer at the bedside of a sick child for whom the darkness was as terrifying as was the darkness at night for Romans afraid of attack by savages. And it brought to that child, as it has for many through the ages, the comfort and assurance that God's love and mercy overcomes the terrors of darkness—and the things that go "bump" in the night.

What Churchman has not rejoiced in the Baptism of a tiny baby, the blessing of its new life, and its incorporation into the fellowship of God's holy Church? What Churchman does not recall the glow in the face of the young boy or girl who kneels to receive the laying on of the Bishop's hands at Confirmation? Who does not recall the joy of the authoritative statement of the parish priest when he joins a man and a woman in Holy Matrimony: "Those whom God hath joined together let no man put asunder"? Who has not been strengthened by the quietly confident words of the Church's last rite: "I am the resurrection and the life, saith the Lord: he that believeth in me, though he were dead, yet shall he live: and whosoever liveth and believeth in me, shall never die."

Greater than all of those is the Lord's own service—the Holy Communion, the great sacrament which he himself instituted in that night in which he was betrayed. "This do," he said, "in remembrance of me"—and Christians have been doing it, in season and out, for two thousand years, sometimes even at the risk of their lives. They do it in red China where the godless government is trying to stamp out every vestige of human dignity. They will be doing it, no matter what dark times may still lie before the Christian Church, until the last days when in fire and flame the Lord himself shall come again to redeem his faithful remnant.

What other act of worship is so universal in its nature, so appropriate alike to occasions of joy and of sorrow? It may be used at the coronation of an earthly sovereign, the celebration of an occasion of national joy, with a mighty organ and well-trained choir pealing forth the triumphant *Te Deum* of victory; or it may be an act of solemn supplication in time of serious peril or national disaster. It may be celebrated with elaborate ceremony in a cathedral or parish church, or quite simply in a home or at the bedside of a sick communicant.

It may be highly personal in its application, as in the growing practice of celebrating the Eucharist at a wedding, for which a special Collect, Epistle, and Gospel are provided in our Prayer Book; or at the burial of the faithful departed, for which similar provision is made. Our people are gradually learning again to use the Holy Eucharist in those ways Christians did in ages past, learning anew the blessing and strength that come from it. I sincerely hope the time will soon come when it will be the general custom, rather than the exceptional, to solemnize marriages with a joyous celebration of the Holy Communion, with the receiving of the blessed Sacrament as the first act of the newly married couple; and to pay the last respects to our departed loved ones with that service which has fortified them through life and in which we commend their souls to God even as we commit their bodies to the ground.

Holy Communion is appropriate not alone to the great occasions, corporate or personal. In the parish church, Sunday by Sunday and during the week, sometimes early in the morning and sometimes late, the banquet of the Lord is spread at his holy table and the faithful are invited to partake of it. Do we realize what an inestimable privilege that is? There were times in the history of our Church, not too long ago, when the Holy Communion was celebrated infrequently, and then often with a barrenness that would shock the most "low Churchman" of today. We have to thank first the followers of John Wesley, and later the men of the Oxford Movement, for the recovery of a vital part of our heritage. Today there is scarcely a parish or mission of the Episcopal Church in which there is not at least a weekly celebration of the Holy Communion and generally one or more during the week, and in some places even daily. If we lay people would make greater use of this great privilege, our priests would gladly provide even more frequent opportunities. On the other hand, if parish priests would schedule more celebrations, more people would participate actively in the worship of the Church.

I have spoken of the personal aspects of the Holy Communion, of its intense relevance to you and to me, in joy or in sorrow. It must always have that personal application and relevance if we approach the altar not "trusting in our own righteousness, but in [God's] manifold and great mercies." If we receive the Holy Sacrament after proper preparation and with a specific intention, it is always a source of strength to us, but it is also far more than that: the Holy Communion is the corporate act of the whole Church; it is the response of the people of God to the redeeming action of our Lord. A French parish priest makes this quite clear. "Let each parish strive to make its liturgy splendid and full of meaning," he writes. "Let each parish make of itself a real community, devoted to the conquest of souls and united within itself for that single goal." [3]

The great Anglican missionary Bishop of Zanzibar, Frank Weston, reminded the congregation at a Solemn Eucharist that it was not enough to find our Lord at the altar and then fail to recognize him in our daily lives, and in the faces of the people with whom we meet. We dare not leave him in the church, nor try to appropriate him to ourselves. We partake of his life-giving strength that we may take it with us into the world—into the office, the shop, the home, and the school. We are to be his witnesses, as he told the little band of his disciples in almost his last earthly message to them, his witnesses in Jerusalem, and in Judea, and in Samaria, and unto the uttermost parts of the world.

The Christian is expected to be a true witness, one who knows whereof he speaks. We have beheld our Lord in his glory; we have communed with him at the altar of our parish church; we have talked with him in prayer and have listened for his response. If our ears are spiritually opened, we hear him speak to us in the age-old words of the liturgy and in the silence of the soul, "the still, small voice" of God the Holy Spirit. Those who know God in such a way need no pin-downed proofs of his existence or of his concern for his children. As we said in an earlier chapter, they know that their Redeemer lives.

The Church is not an organization of saints, but a community of sinners—which is to say, a community of men and women like you and me. Are there hypocrites within it, as it is charged by our detractors? Of course! And if we are honest, we must admit that often we are among them. When we use the expression "the Communion of Saints," we are not claiming that all Christians are good; indeed, one has only to read the life of any saint to recognize his consciousness of his own sin. What makes one a saint is not his freedom from sin, much less from temptation, but one's constant striving and determination by God's help to resist temptation and to overcome sin.

Alan Paton puts it beautifully in his "Meditation for a Young Boy Confirmed":

> This kneeling, this singing, this reading from ancient books,
> This acknowledgement that the burden is intolerable, this promise
>   of amendment,
> This humble access, this putting out of the hands,
> This taking of bread and wine, this return to your place not
>   glancing about you,
> This solemn acceptance and the thousand sins that will follow it,
> This thousand sins and the repenting of them,
> This dedication and this apostasy, this apostasy and this restoration,
> This thousand restorations and this thousand apostacies,
> Take and accept them all, be not affronted nor dismayed by them,
> They are a net of holes to capture essence, a shell to house the
>   thunder of an ocean,
> A discipline of petty acts to catch Creation, a rune of words to hold
>   One Living Word,
> A ladder built by men of sticks and stones, whereby they hope to
>   reach to heaven.[4]

Or we may express it in the Bishop's prayer at the consecration of a church:

Blessed be thy Name, O Lord, that it hath pleased thee to put it into the hearts of thy servants to appropriate and devote this house to thy honour and worship; and grant that all who shall enjoy the benefit of this pious work, may show forth their thankfulness, by making a right use of it, to the glory of thy blessed Name; through Jesus Christ our Lord. *Amen.* (Prayer Book, p. 566)

"Dig We Must"

CHAPTER SIX

I HAVE always rather liked the slogan of New York's Consolidated Edison Company: "Dig we must, for a growing New York." You see it on innumerable street barriers (particularly innumerable when you are watching a taxi meter) behind which public utility workers lay pipes and wires, or otherwise disturb traffic in the interest of improvements for the future.

So it can be with the Christian religion. If we are to make it the living and present power in our own lives and in the life of our communities and the world, we cannot be content with the pavement on the surface but must dig deep down inside ourselves (where the cables are) for a truer Christianity and a better life.

When the first two Russian cosmonauts orbited the earth, they reported on return that they had looked around carefully but had not seen God sitting on a cloud with Jesus Christ at his right side. They seemed to think that would be a devastating answer to the claims of Christianity, but any well-informed Christian could have told them that it would have been much more devastating if they had observed such a phenomenon! It is not certain that Christians ever thought that God literally sat in some localized place a few miles above the earth to regulate the movement of the sun, moon, and stars, to cast thunderbolts and send rain and lightning, snow and sleet, down upon the hapless residents of the earth. Our ancestors were not so naive as some modern writers depict them. Such a concept actually fits better with the paganism of ancient Greece than with the Christian knowledge of God as the loving Father of all creation.

54

I have news for the Russians. Even if they get to the moon or to some distant star, they will be no closer to the kingdom of heaven. Their brethren who have remained loyal to the Russian Orthodox Church could have told them the same news if they had listened. Two thousand years ago our Lord Jesus Christ spoke plainly on the subject: "The kingdom of God," he said, "is within you."

One of our most popular contemporary novelists, J. D. Salinger, in his rough and ready way, shows vividly just how remarkable that news is even today. In his *Franny and Zooey* he has a scene in which Zooey reproaches Franny for her sentimental attitude toward religion and for the way she seems to separate God from ordinary life. He reminds Franny that "Jesus realized there is *no* separation from God," and that he said that the kingdom of God is inside us.

So we have to dig down deep inside ourselves to find the kingdom of God. It is a painful operation—and it is not easy—to find the kingdom of God in our own hearts. Probably we'll find a good many other things, some of them rather nasty and unpleasant, before we discover the kingdom of God—and alas, we may never discover it!

For one thing, we shall probably find that the kingdom of the devil is also within us. Any psychiatrist can tell you that the warfare between God and the devil is not something that happened billions of years ago in some region of outer space but that it goes on today inside the human heart and mind and soul. The psychiatrists might not put it that way, for, like theologians, they have their own brand of technical jargon. Yet the gist of statements from both kinds of specialists is much the same: good and evil, adjustment and maladjustment, saintliness and sinfulness—call them what you will—are at war within each one of us for the possession of our soul or for the domination of our selves. Words and phrases change with the changing of patterns of thought, but the concept remains the same, and the inner warfare continues.

What power do we bring to that inner conflict? Christianity says God gave to man free will, the power to choose between good and evil. We exercise that power in every choice we make. We can fight on either side—the side of God, or the side of the devil—but we cannot remain neutral. God gave us the ability to choose but not the prerogative to stand aside and take no part in the battle. "He that is not with me is against me." It is as simple as that.

The Prayer Book collect for the Second Sunday in Lent puts it plainly:

Almighty God, who seest that we have no power of ourselves to help ourselves; Keep us both outwardly in our bodies, and inwardly in our souls; that we may be defended from all adversities which may happen to the body, and from all evil thoughts which may assault and hurt the soul; through Jesus Christ our Lord. *Amen.*

"No power of ourselves to help ourselves" may sound negative and fatalistic, but it really isn't that way at all: we do have that freedom of choice, the power to enlist God's help and to fight on his side, or the power to reject him and thus join the forces that fight against him. Moreover, he has promised us that if we call upon him in faith he will defend us "from all adversities which may happen to the body and from all evil thoughts which may assault and hurt the soul." We can count upon God to do his part, but only if we do ours.

Some years ago a series of books appeared under the title *This I Believe*. It was a collection of statements by various people, originally broadcast over the radio and published in newspapers, which gave the viewpoints of individual writers. One reviewer noted that humanism undoubtedly was the strongest note of this book, and quoted Pearl Buck's statement: "I feel no need for any other faith than my faith in human beings." He also quoted Harold Taylor, then president of Sarah Lawrence College: "I believe in people, sheer unadulterated humanity."

In the light of history and of the contemporary world, how anyone can express faith in humanity without reference to God is more than I can understand! One need not go back to the barbarism of Genghis Khan or Nero; he has only to recall the ovens of Buchenwald, or to read the record of the latest Communist outrages in Cuba or Viet-Nam or Laos, or the newspaper accounts of the latest gangland killing in our own country to refute belief in unredeemed humanity. Evil exists with us as well as with our enemies, and our enemies are not exclusively evil, nor we exclusively good.

I believe in man not because of man's own goodness but rather because he is God's creature, and because God, through Jesus Christ, has saved man from his unredeemed humanity. Therefore I can believe in man only because I first believe in God the Father, who created him, in God the Son, who redeems him, and in God the Holy Spirit who can lift him above his mere humanity and make him to be called the child of God. Only God can save man from humanity—or inhumanity.

If I believe in God, I must also believe in the Church because it is the continuing life of Jesus Christ today. At the font, in Holy Baptism, infants are signed with the cross and admitted to the fellowship of Christ's religion. At the altar, in Holy Communion, men and women receive his body and his blood, as he promised, for the strengthening of their souls and to enable them better to do his will in whatever walk of life he has called them to in his world.

When our Lord said to his first disciples, "Go ye into all the world and teach all nations," he was speaking not only to the inner circle of the Apostles, or to the bishops and other clergy who would be their successors throughout the ages; he was speaking to all of his followers, and he speaks still to all of us, clergy and laity alike. I think it was Archbishop Temple who once said, "The priest stands for God before the congregation, but the congregation stands for God before the whole world." That puts a huge task upon us laymen because the world will not judge Christianity by the clergy, but by us, who profess and call ourselves Christians, and how we show forth our faith in our daily lives.

Human nature, unredeemed by God, does not have an especially good or notable record in the pages of history.

Left to himself David had Uriah killed, that he might take Uriah's wife.

Left to themselves, men crucified Jesus—but God intervened with the glorious news of the resurrection.

Left to ourselves a hundred years ago in the American Civil War, brothers killed brothers and devastated our country.

Left to themselves in World War II, the leaders of a supposedly Christian country developed the grisly industry of exterminating Jews by the millions.

Left to ourselves tomorrow, we may wipe out civilization with the powerful weapons of mass destruction now neatly stockpiled in the armories of the United States and Soviet Russia.

In the past, by the providence of God, we have always stopped short of complete self-destruction, but more wars have been brought to an end by weariness than by repentance. Will we turn to God in time for him to pull our chestnuts out of an atomic fire? That is the present, terrible question.

God works through men to accomplish his purposes—not just the great and mighty and powerful men, but all men, you and me. We may choose between good and evil—and that choice was never more important than it is today. The future of the human race depends on that choice. It always has; it always will. That is where our religion became quite certainly a matter of life or death for us.

If the Christian religion is really that crucial, why does it seem so unimportant to millions of people, including, if we would be quite honest, ourselves? I suggest that it is largely because of some quite common misconceptions of what religion is and of its place in our lives. I should like to touch upon just three such false conceptions.

The first one might be called the legalistic concept. Many people think religion is primarily a set of rules handed down by God or developed by an impersonal hierarchy throughout the ages—a code that is perhaps outmoded or outgrown today. One cannot honestly say that the Ten Commandments are outworn or outmoded, although they certainly are not fashionable today. We tend to resent them, I think, because they are authoritarian, negative, and arbitrary. "Thou shalt not . . ." is not the popular way to begin a statement in these days of "positive thinking" and permissiveness. We don't talk to our children that way, and we resent the idea that God should talk to us in that way.

Whatever the popular understanding, religion is not primarily a set of rules. It is basically a matter of relationships—our relationship with God and our relationship with our fellow men. That is what our Lord was saying when he summarized the Law and the Prophets in three sentences:

Thou shalt love the Lord thy God with all thy heart, and with all thy soul, and with all thy mind. This is the first and great commandment. And the second is like unto it; Thou shalt love thy neighbour as thyself.

There is the true concept of the Christian religion. It is quite positive and creative, not at all negative and legalistic. It is, in fact, a religion of love.

The second misconception is that religion is a hypocritical thing, a matter of mere sentiment, summed up in the phrase "holier than thou." That concept, which we got from the Puritan colonists, is certainly not borne out by the New Testament. The early Christians were not "holier than thou"; it was the chief priests and scribes who merited the description, and they were the ones who were instrumental in putting our Lord to death! The Christian Church was not and is not a society of saints, but rather a congregation of sinners who know they are sinners but who are trying to overcome their sins. The human side of the Church is balanced by the divine side, in which the Church can properly be described as the Body of Christ. Once again we see that Christ works within us and that without his help we have "no power of ourselves to help ourselves."

The third and most dangerous misconception of religion is that it is a matter of opinion, or is optional—something we can take or leave; and, if we do take it, it is for our spare time. Nothing could be farther from the truth. Every man has a religion. The question is whether his religion is good or bad, true or false.

Caesar had religion—the religion of ambition.

Hitler had religion—the religion of power.

Khrushchev has religion—the religion of dialectic materialism.

Castro has religion—the religion of pride.

America has religion—the religion of "the American way of life."

Every man worships someone or something, and he becomes more and more like that which he worships. If his religion is ambition, power, pride, or the accumulation of possessions, he becomes more ambitious, more power seeking, more intolerant, more greedy. If his religion is love, he will become more tolerant, more understanding, more generous, more loving. Christianity is the religion of love; its simplest definition of God is its three great big words: God is love.

Because God is love he is to us a loving Father—not a sternly implacable Father nor a weakly sentimental Father, but one who loves and cares for his children with infinite patience and wisdom. Like a loving Father he showers gifts upon his children; and since he is a wise Father, he expects us to use his gifts wisely as they are given.

The first of God's gifts is the gift of time. The author of *The Cloud of Unknowing,* one of the great spiritual classics, reminds us that "time was made for man and not man for time . . . therefore take heed how you spend your time for there is nothing more precious than time." How often, when we are asked to do something, we say "I don't have time for it"—yet we manage to find time for things we really want to do.

Today, with the regulated hours of most industries and businesses, we have more control over our time than ever before, but most people, even in the days when working hours were long, had surprising control over their time—enough to apportion it much as they might wish. Alexander lived only twenty-five years, but he found time to conquer the world: in the same short span of years others have found time to drink themselves to death.

God gives us time, and he expects us to use it for our benefit and for the benefit of the community in which we live. In the modern world we have more of that precious commodity at our disposal than ever before; in fact, one of the great problems of modern society is the ineffectual use of time. If we took half as much trouble in budgeting our time as some of us do in budgeting our money, we should find that we have time for everything that we want to do—a time for work, a time for rest, a time for prayer, a time to be with our families, a time to give to some constructive work of Church or charity. Time is God's gift; let us use it wisely.

The second of God's gifts is the gift of work. In the early books of the Bible work was considered to be drudgery. The punishment of Adam when he was expelled from the Garden of Eden was that he and his descendants would have to earn their living by the sweat of their brow. The New Testament, however, as in the parable of the laborers in the vineyard, regards honest work as good in itself. "The laborer is worthy of his hire."

There is nothing degrading in honest work or in the sweat of the brow. Work that is honest and constructive and useful to society is good work. Work makes the world go round. The laborer, the office worker, the housewife, the teacher, should take just as much pride in a good job well done as the artist or poet or sculptor. It is the rich man with nothing to do, or the loafer, or the playboy, who is most subject to boredom, idleness, and eventually to despair, sometimes leading to suicide. Be proud of your work and do it to the best of your ability, for work is the gift of God. Thomas a Kempis summed it up when he said: "He does much that loves much. He does much that does a thing well. He does well that serves the community rather than his own will."

We are called to work in two different ways—one in which we earn our living, and one in which we strive to be better human beings. Each is important, and each requires our best efforts.

Man is a social animal—but sometimes he seems to be more animal than social. Is that because he has trouble with one of the strangest precepts of religion, the Second Commandment of the *Shema,* the summary of the Law—that we love our neighbors as ourselves? First of all, how can I love myself when I know what a bundle of contradictions I am—good and bad, strong and weak, smart and dumb? Some people get so discouraged when they look inside themselves that they lose all confidence, and sometimes all hope, with the resultant danger of loss of personality and surrender to the ultimate sin of self-destruction. A Christian must have respect for himself as a child of God, before he can respect, to say nothing of love, his neighbor.

And who is my neighbor? The Pharisees tried to trap Jesus on that question, but Jesus refused to walk into the trap. He answered with the parable of the Good Samaritan—the point of which is that any man, even a man of a different race or nation or religion or political philosophy, is your neighbor. To the Pharisees, the Samaritan was a foreigner, a heretic, a subversive character; but he was nonetheless a man, and he had the instincts of human decency. As such, he was a neighbor, to be respected and loved as oneself. How much easier it would be to solve our problems of personal relations, of civil rights, of national and international tensions, if we could learn to approach them in the Christian spirit.

Life is not all work, however, and God gives us also the gift of leisure. It has been truly said that the right use of leisure is one of the great problems of contemporary society. One has only to look at the statistics for drinking, gambling, television, movies, hobbies, and idle entertainment to see the large proportion of time, money, and substance wasted by modern Americans in their leisure occupations.

It is not that these things are evil in themselves. Used in moderation, they are often beneficial. It is the undue preoccupation of time and effort going into trivial amusements which indicate the barrenness and futility of many people's lives. People talk about "killing time," as if time were an enemy that somehow has to be done away with.

God expects us to use his gift of leisure wisely. It is right to use a proportion of it for rest, recreation, and fun; but there is still so much of it that most of us could use more constructively. We can devote some of it to visiting the sick, the widows, and the fatherless —a scriptural recommendation that has almost passed out of our contemporary customs. We can devote it to fostering true friendship and understanding—an art that is increasingly rare. We can devote it to a variety of good works, not necessarily "religious" in the narrow sense, but in the spirit of obedience to the twofold injunction to love God and to love our fellow man.

Loneliness is an affliction from which modern men and women suffer, perhaps to a greater degree than ever before. In the midst of the pressures of an impersonal and industrial society, we have largely lost touch with nature and with our fellow human beings. In so doing, we lose touch with God and we surrender something of the fullness of our humanity. Most of us would do well to rethink the use of our leisure time and to consider whether it cannot be used more creatively to the glory of God and to our own spiritual benefit. Indeed, if we are grateful to God for his gifts of time, work, and leisure, how can we do otherwise than try to use them in his honor and glory?

I have tried to suggest some ways in which we can dig into our own interior life, as dig we must if we are to see ourselves truly as God sees us. I have touched upon only a few of the things that we may find if we dig conscientiously. You will find many others, some of them far more important than those I have mentioned, if you take time now and then for a little spiritual probing, a little effort to make an inventory of your spiritual assets and liabilities, a little effort to recognize that we have "no power of ourselves to help ourselves" and to see that God will help us if we but try to help ourselves.

A generation ago, men could and did believe in a world of progress, one which, because of increasing education, the unfolding of miracles in science, and the invention of more and better gadgets, was sure to get better and better as time went on. Today that kind of shallow optimism is gone. We have learned that education without spiritual growth can often do more harm than good and that better gadgets do not necessarily lead to a better life. Above all, the advance of the physical sciences, culminating in the H-bomb and bacteriological warfare, has knocked the props from under mankind and left us with less feeling of security than ever in history. Now we have the threat of an even more obscene weapon—one that will kill people but leave their buildings intact. What could be a greater inversion of human values than that?

The pushing back of the frontiers of science has shown us the human race emerging from the darkness of the primeval chaos, only to head for an all-enveloping blaze of global self-destruction. Was it for such an end that God created man in his own likeness?

At the present time (or at any other time, for that matter) only faith in God gives any real meaning to life. Fortunately, we have the sure and certain warrant for such faith. We have it in the eternal word of God, recorded in the Holy Scriptures and lived by saintly men and women in every age, transmitted through the Church which has survived destruction of more than one civilization, and nourished by the bread of life given to us by Christ himself in the sacrament of the Holy Communion. There, and there alone, is to be found the meaning of life, the reason for our being, and the hope of our future, both individually and for the human race.

As one layman to other laymen, therefore, I say that this is our task: to carry Christ out from the altar and the Church into the marketplace and the home so that men coming into contact with us in our daily occupations may know that we have walked with Christ and may, through us, learn something of his loving kindness, his power and great might, his ability to lead us through all crises of life, until at last we come into his nearer presence and hear his words, "Well done, thou good and faithful servant."

The General Convention

CHAPTER SEVEN

THE Episcopal Church may well be proud of its General Convention. It is one of the ablest and most democratic assemblies of any American religious body. At the same time it has a built-in system of checks and balances that effectively prevent hasty or ill-considered action that would jeopardize the constitution of the Church or the integrity of the Book of Common Prayer, and thus it is not subject to the varying winds of doctrinal whims or passing innovations.

The General Convention meets every three years and is many things to many people. To most Churchmen it is a great rally of Episcopalians, an opportunity to take part with great numbers in splendid services of public worship, to hear and often to meet the Presiding Bishop and other church leaders, and to catch a glimpse of the Church at work on a national and international scale. The significance of that aspect of the General Convention should not be underestimated. Time and again the layman whose only knowledge of the Church has been at the level of his own parish or mission, or at best at the diocesan level, sees the Church as something much larger and more far-reaching than he had suspected; and he is a better Churchman for the experience.

To the faithful, hard-working, devoted women of the Church, the triennial meeting of the Episcopal Churchwomen, held at the same time and place as the sessions of the bishops and deputies, is a high point of their church experience. There the women, elected through parochial and diocesan machinery, meet for devotion, inspiration, deliberation, and action on matters of common concern, and for planning their national program for the next three years.

Most important is the in-gathering of the United Thank Offering, made up of their gifts through the familiar blue boxes into which they have placed so many dimes and dollars with thankful hearts for many blessings, large and small. Moreover, through their elected national officers, and in consultation with the Presiding Bishop and National Council, they determine the allocation of those funds for capital expenditures in the mission field, for the support of women workers, and for a wide variety of good works that would not otherwise be possible.

To various Church organizations, official and unofficial, the General Convention offers an opportunity for national meetings, or for displays and exhibits to publicize their activities and to gain new members or supporters for their particular concerns.

To the Church's young people it is often the occasion for a special rally or for a youth weekend, at which they not only get to know one another and have a good time but also to learn much about their Church and to extend their religious horizons. They are the future bishops and priests, vestrymen, and women workers. The General Convention may awaken in them the seeds of a dormant vocation.

To the secular press, radio, and television, the General Convention is an event of sufficient importance to justify top-level coverage, and increasingly they send their most experienced men and women to report it. In past years that was not always the case; newspapers had little interest in such assemblies, except to report the sensational; and readers were likely to gain the impression that the Episcopal Church was about to split in two or that the main purpose of the General Convention was to serve as a forum for heresy, schism, and sensationalism. There has been great improvement, especially in the past two decades, in the responsible reporting of national church assemblies; the vote of appreciation to the media of mass communication customarily adopted at the close of a General Convention is not a perfunctory gesture but a grateful recognition of this fact.

To publishers, booksellers, and dealers in vestments, brassware, and church furnishings and supplies of all kinds, the General Convention is an opportunity to display their wares, to learn of new needs and opportunities, and to establish personal relations with customers and prospects.

To Church colleges and seminaries, the General Convention is an occasion for reunion dinners, for making new acquaintances and renewing old friendships, for presenting their programs and needs to the church public upon whom they rely for interest and support.

Those and many other by-products of the General Convention and the triennial meeting of the women of the Church are not to be lightly regarded, as they often are by those who would "streamline" the Convention and "eliminate the side-shows" in the supposed interest of efficiency or economy, or because they fear any suggestion of controversy that might disturb the even tenor of the Church's complacent way of life. That there are such disturbing factors there is no doubt. To cite but two of them: the Church League for Industrial Democracy in the 1930's and the Episcopal Society for Cultural and Racial Unity in the 1960's were organized and promoted for the specific purpose of disturbing the complacency of Church people, and they did their job with surprising success. The Church would be the poorer if it did not have, in every age, those who were dissatisfied with the status quo and determined to awaken the Church from the torpor and self-satisfaction that is its constant temptation.

The heart of the General Convention—in fact, the only body that is entitled to that name—is the Church's bicameral legislature, which consists of the House of Bishops and the House of Clerical and Lay Deputies. In most parts of the Anglican Communion, as in Catholic tradition generally, such a legislature is termed a General Synod, and is the advisory and executive agency of the Archbishop, metropolitan, or primate of a province of a national Church. For some reason—probably because of the eighteenth century prejudices against English institutions and organizations—the Episcopal

Church has eschewed the title and office of Archbishop, as well as the traditional name *synod* for its national and diocesan governing bodies. (A few dioceses have courageously restored the name *synod,* but the general term in use is *diocesan convention,* and in missionary districts, *convocation.*)

The General Convention, however, has more actual powers than most national synods or convocations (the term used in the provinces of Canterbury and York), or the Church Assembly of the Church of England. The Church, meeting in General Convention, adopted its constitution in 1785, and set forth the American version of the Book of Common Prayer in 1789. By joint action in two successive triennial sessions, it can amend the constitution, and frequently does so. In like manner it can revise or amend the Book of Common Prayer, and did so in 1892 and in 1928.

Other actions of the General Convention may be taken in a single session. Most important is the enactment, amendment, or repeal of canons, in accordance with the Church's constitution. Canons, from the word *rule,* are the laws by which the Church is governed not only nationally but on diocesan and parish levels. (Diocesan conventions may also adopt and amend their own constitutions and canons, but they may not contravene the constitution and canons of the national Church.)

The Church's constitution and canons are unfamiliar to most laymen, although the laity are governed by them in their church relations just as members of clergy are. Among the canonical provisions most important to lay people are those that define their status as "baptized persons," "communicants," and "communicants in good standing" (curiously, not adopted until 1961), those that define their marital status in the eyes of the Church, those that establish the relationship of rector and vestry, the right of parishioners to elect wardens and vestrymen, to demand and receive letters of transfer from one parish to another, and so on. Probably few laymen realize that they are required by canon "Of the Due Observance of Sundays" to "celebrate and keep the Lord's day, commonly called Sunday, by regular participation in the public worship of the Church, by hearing the Word of God read and taught, and by other acts of devotion, and works of charity, using all godly and sober conversation." Even more binding, since the Prayer Book has the force of constitutional law, is the layman's "bounden duty"— "to worship God every Sunday in his Church, and to work and pray and give for the spread of Christ's kingdom," as set forth in the Second Office of Instruction. If he would achieve and maintain his status as a communicant in good standing, he must also receive Holy Communion at least three times a year, "unless for good cause prevented."

The Church is chary of inflicting penalties on laymen who do not observe its laws. Only if he is "a notorious evil liver," or if he deliberately contracts a marriage contrary to the Church's laws may a layman be excommunicated; and even in such cases there is charitable provision for his reinstatement at the discretion of his bishop or by decision of an ecclesiastical court acting with the bishop.

In addition to matters relating to the Prayer Book and the constitution and canons, the General Convention has final authority in all matters concerning the program and budget of the Episcopal Church, its relation to other religious bodies, its administration and policy, requirements for theological education and ordination, its national requirements in Christian education, missions, social relations, and the like. In most such matters, the General Convention lays down general lines of policy, and the Presiding Bishop and National Council are the executive and administrative agency. Some matters, important for administration as well as policy planning, are entrusted to joint commissions and committees that hold sessions between conventions.

The General Convention is also the only official national agency for resolutions declaring the policy of the Episcopal Church in such important matters as national and international problems—war and peace, capital punishment, race relations, and the like. It cannot, however, compel the consciences of its people, or even dictate the action of local parishes and dioceses in such matters, though it can exert a powerful influence upon them. It may be considered as expressing the corporate conscience of the Church, or at least of the majority of informed Churchmen, but it has no power to bind the personal conscience of any church member.

A good example was the resolution of General Convention in 1958 condemning capital punishment, which stands as the most authoritative statement of the Church at the national level. There are, however, many Churchmen—myself included—who believe that the death penalty can be justified, especially in cases where mass murder, atrocity, genocide, or high treason is involved. No one, I am sure, will venture to "read me out of the Church" because I think the world is better off without such a criminal mass murderer as Adolf Eichmann.

My first General Convention was the one held in New Orleans in 1925. I was not a deputy but was assigned to cover certain aspects of it for *The Living Church*. I had just completed my senior year at Harvard, but I was a few credits short of graduation, and had to return to complete my work for graduation the following February. Unexpectedly, my experience in reporting the General Convention helped me to complete my requirements. One of the questions on my examination in a course on modern government was to describe in detail the operation of a legislative assembly. I took the General Convention as my subject, and told exactly how the Episcopal Church handled its legislation. My professor summoned me to say that he had meant a legislative body in a state or national government. I pulled the printed examination sheet from my pocket and pointed out that the question said merely "a legislative assembly," and that my paper had clearly shown that the General Convention was that. He had to admit the logic of my contention, and since he knew nothing of the government of the Church, he gave me the benefit of the doubt and awarded me an *A* for my paper!

The first General Convention to which I went as a deputy took place in 1934 at Atlantic City. My father had died in 1932. He, and his father before him, had been elected by the Diocese of Milwaukee to represent it in the House of Deputies at every General Convention since 1884. Since I had succeeded my father as editor of *The Living Church,* I suppose the diocese simply wanted to carry on the tradition, even though I was only twenty-nine years old at the time of my election.

The 1934 convention met in an atmosphere of gloom, despite its holiday setting. Financially, the Church was staggering from five years of depression. Parishes and missions were laboring under mountains of mortgage debts which had been incurred in the lavish predepression days. Missionary enterprises, at home and abroad, were being closed for lack of funds. Along with the financial gloom, a shadow of spiritual darkness seemed to hang over the deliberations. The committee on budget and program, meeting long hours of the day and far into the evening, could only recommend cuts in every missionary district—retrenchment, retirement, retreat.

Out of the darkness came a gleam of light, destined to make of the 1934 General Convention a real turning point in the history of the Church. Concluding the report of the budget committee, following rows of discouraging facts and figures, came the recommendation for a joint commission to plan "a definite forward movement in the Church with the object of reinvigorating its life and rehabilitating parish, diocese and the general Church."

The General Convention seized upon that recommendation, and unanimously approved the appointment of a Forward Movement Commission. The Presiding Bishop and the president of the House of Deputies appointed a carefully selected body of five bishops, five presbyters (General Convention term for priests), and ten laymen under the chairmanship of Henry Wise Hobson, Bishop of Southern Ohio, to undertake the task of surveying the whole Church, diocese by diocese, to determine its needs and to recommend ways of turning retreat into advance, defeat into victory.

Bishop Hobson became the chairman of the commission and his leadership soon revealed that his middle name was well chosen. I was appointed to the commission—its youngest and least experienced member. The Forward Movement proved to be a hard class in the school of experience during the next six years. Under the able leadership of Bishop Hobson, its members traveled the length and breadth of the Church, talking with bishops, priests, and laymen, surveying its needs and helping to plan programs which looked forward both financially and spiritually. At the same time the commission began publishing the valuable booklet of daily Bible readings, *Forward Day by Day,* a publication which still is an important part of the life of the Church. The commission itself no longer exists, but the publication of valuable teaching material continues under the imprint of Forward Movement Publications.

Subsequent General Conventions have generally been more optimistic than that of 1934, and each has given further impetus to the work of the Church and its adjustment to contemporary conditions. There have been setbacks, however. In the General Convention of 1946, the Commission on Approaches to Unity proposed a plan for merger with the Presbyterians, a plan many considered hasty and ill-thought-out. Rejection of the plan caused the Presbyterians to feel that the Episcopalians had been guilty of bad faith, and constructive conversations between the two churches were suspended for fifteen years. Meanwhile the Presbyterians were able to enlarge their own inner unity; and when expanded conversations were authorized in 1961 to include the Methodists, the United Church of Christ, and others, it proved possible to begin anew on a firmer basis of mutual fellowship and understanding.

It was my privilege in 1961 to be elected president of the House of Deputies, the second layman to be chosen for that office; Supreme Court Justice Owen Roberts, of Pennsylvania, was the first. He presided over the stormy sessions of 1946. Greater harmony prevailed at the 1961 General Convention, though it was not without its exciting moments. The greatest controversy was over the National Council of Churches and our membership in it. The conflict was resolved, at least for the moment, by the authorization of a committee, under the Joint Commission on Ecumenical Relations, to make a thorough study of the situation and report to the 1964 Convention.

For the most part, the 1961 General Convention was a happy one. Its chief accomplishments were the ratification of full communion with the Philippine Independent Church and two small churches in Spain and Portugal, and the growing recognition of the importance of constructive church action in the fields of industry and race relations.

For my part, I thoroughly enjoyed presiding over such a distinguished and sometimes turbulent body, which is nearly half again as large as the House of Representatives in Washington. Members occasionally tried to entangle the new president in parliamentary red tape or to take him for an ecclesiastical ride; but I felt that they were all my friends, and we weathered the storms together without too much difficulty.

Far-reaching proposals will be made for the reorganization of the General Convention, to make it less unwieldy and to enable it to use its time more effectively. In the interests of efficiency that is important; but such changes also tend to make the House of Deputies less personal. Time was when the House was small enough, and its sessions long enough, to permit real oratory and reasoned argument to formulate decisions. Now the work must be done mostly through written reports, often only hastily read, and by the device of open hearings on the more important questions.

There are two kinds of church people who are not considered eligible for representation in the General Convention. One group is that of deacons, who are not eligible as either clerical or lay deputies. I am not overconcerned about deacons, however, since most of them go on to the priesthood and will, in due course, be eligible for election to the House of Deputies. The other and far larger group is the women of the Church. The women, thank God, will remain women, and we would not have it otherwise. Women are barred from election to the House by an interpretation of the Constitution, which may or may not be the only possible interpretation, but is the one that has so far prevailed.

When the question of eligibility of women comes up in the House of Deputies at the next General Convention, as it has at every General Convention for the past 18 or 20 years, I hope the deputies will have the sound judgment to amend the Constitution (if it cannot be reinterpreted) to make women unquestionably eligible for election.

The old argument that if women were allowed to sit in the House of Deputies, they would soon outnumber the men and the men would not take their fair share in the work of the Church, is not only untrue but is an unwarranted slander upon the loyalty of the men of the Church. That it is untrue is proved by the fact that where women are eligible to sit in diocesan conventions, they have never taken the leadership away from the men, nor have they done so in such ecclesiastical bodies as the Church Assembly in England. It is slanderous because the loyalty of the kind of laymen who are elected to the General Convention is beyond question. If it were true that the men would leave the leadership to the women, it would be a sad day for the Church. The truth of the matter is that men and women are equally loyal communicants of the Church, and the practice of segregation by sex in General Convention is no more admirable than that of segregation by race or color.

Other reforms may be desirable also, not only in the House of Deputies but also in the House of Bishops, which threatens increasingly to be controlled by retired bishops and suffragan bishops, who lack the responsibilities of jurisdiction in their dioceses. Perhaps also the name might be changed to General Synod and the Presiding Bishop be given the traditional title, jurisdiction, and duties of an Archbishop or Primate.

On the whole, however, the General Convention is probably the most democratic and well-organized ecclesiastical body in any hierarchical church. I would not like to see it greatly changed either in the direction of flexibility or of rigidity. I would, however, like to see the House of Deputies given a more proportionately representational basis if it could be done without increasing its size; and perhaps some of the responsibilities of the General Convention could be delegated to regional synods in the several provinces at home and abroad.

Almighty and everlasting God, who by thy Holy Spirit didst preside in the Council of the blessed Apostles, and hast promised, through thy Son Jesus Christ, to be with thy Church to the end of the world; We beseech thee to be with the Council of thy Church assembled in thy Name and Presence. Save [its members] from all error, ignorance, pride, and prejudice; and of thy great mercy vouchsafe, we beseech thee, so to direct, sanctify, and govern them in their work, by the mighty power of the Holy Ghost, that the comfortable Gospel of Christ may be truly preached, truly received, and truly followed, in all places, to the breaking down the kingdom of sin, Satan, and death; till at length the whole of thy dispersed sheep, being gathered into one fold, shall become partakers of everlasting life; through the merits and death of Jesus Christ our Saviour. *Amen.*

                                              (Prayer Book, page 36)

What about Christian Unity?

CHAPTER EIGHT

TALK of Christian unity is widespread today. In almost every Church and religious body there has been during the past half-century a growing awareness that the separateness of Christian religious bodies is not our Lord's will, or true to the concept of *"One,* Holy, Catholic, Apostolic Church." Particularly is that true in the United States, which has some 250 or more religious bodies, all claiming the name "Christian," yet all maintaining their separate organizations and identities—a situation which seems to many to be a scandalous betrayal of the very nature of the Christian Church. Our Lord himself prayed that his followers might be united in one body, even as he and the Father are one; and he prophesied that "there shall be one fold, and one shepherd" (John 10:16).

The unity of Christendom has been the principal concern since 1920 of the Faith and Order Movement, now a part of the World Council of Churches. The movement had its origin in the General Convention of the Episcopal Church, when the Rev. William T. Manning, then Rector of Trinity Parish, New York, and later Bishop of New York, introduced a resolution in the House of Deputies calling for a World Council on Faith and Order, to which all Christian Churches were invited to send delegates. Adopted by the General Convention of the Episcopal Church, the resolution met with immediate response on the part of other Christian communions throughout the world and resulted in the first World Conference of Faith and Order at Lausanne, Switzerland, in 1927. At that conference most of the historic churches of Christendom were represented, including several of the Eastern Orthodox churches. The Roman Catholic Church was invited to join at the outset but declined to do so.

Subsequent World Councils on Faith and Order, each with a larger and more representative group of participating churches, met at Edinburgh, Scotland, in 1937; at Lund, Sweden, in 1952; and at Montreal, Canada, in 1963. At Lund there were unofficial observers from the Roman Catholic Church, and at Montreal there were official Roman Catholic observers, although that Church continued to decline full participation in the conference.

Over the years the Faith and Order Movement has developed a platform of Christian unity, which was made official through the adoption of the report on unity at the World Council Assembly in New Delhi, India, in 1961. It is summarized in the following paragraph, and indicates the nature of the unity sought by the participating churches:

We believe that the unity which is both God's will and his gift to his Church is being made visible as all in each place, who are baptized into Jesus Christ and confess him as Lord and Saviour, are brought by the Holy Spirit into ONE fully committed fellowship, holding the one apostolic faith, preaching the one Gospel, breaking the one bread, joining in common prayer, and having a corporate life reaching out in witness and service to all and who at the same time are united with the whole Christian fellowship in all places and all ages in such wise that ministry and members are accepted by all, and that all can act and speak together as occasion requires for the tasks to which God calls his people.

The Anglican Communion also has its platform for Christian unity known as the Chicago-Lambeth Quadrilateral. The statement grew out of a resolution approved by the General Convention of 1886 held in Chicago, later adopted by the Lambeth Conference in 1888, and subsequently embodied in an "appeal to all Christian peoples" in 1920. As recently as the General Convention of 1961, the Episcopal Church reaffirmed the four points of the Quadrilateral (according to the stronger wording of the Chicago original) as the only basis on which this church could hold conversations with other churches on the subject of Christian unity, and it has in fact been the basis for intercommunion with certain non-Anglican churches.

Although the Quadrilateral has been stated in several varying versions, the four points remain basically unchanged. They are:

1. The Holy Scripture of the Old and New Testaments.
2. The Nicene and Apostles' Creeds.
3. The Gospel Sacraments of Baptism and Holy Communion.
4. The Historic Episcopate, or the Apostolic Ministry of Bishops, Priests and Deacons.

The first three of the points need little elaboration since we share them more or less with all the historic Christianity, both Catholic and Protestant. There are, of course, differences of interpretation of the Bible and of the two major sacraments, and differences of use of the two historic creeds. It is the fourth point, however, the historic episcopate or the apostolic ministry, which has hitherto proved a stumbling block to conversations or negotiations with Protestant bodies which have lost that essential element of Catholic order.

Episcopalians have never claimed that their Church is the one and only true Church. (As the story goes, an Episcopalian was asked if there were salvation outside the Episcopal Church, and replied, "Oh, yes, of course. But no gentleman would take advantage of it.") There is a sense in which we have no faith of our own, as we profess loyalty not to "Episcopalianism" but to the universal Catholic Church.

The title page of the Prayer Book says, "The Book of Common Prayer and Administration of the Sacraments and Other Rites and Ceremonies of the Church, according to the use of the Protestant Episcopal Church in the United States of America." We are not baptized into the Episcopal Church but rather into *The Church,* wherein we become members of Christ and heirs of the kingdom of heaven. When the bishop confirms us, he does not confirm us as Episcopalians but, acting by virtue of his authority as a bishop of

the universal Church, he admits us to full communicant membership in *The Church*. Nowhere in the Prayer Book is there any
indication that our membership is in an exclusive part of the
Church, except in the Offices of Ordination where the deacon,
priest, or bishop must swear allegiance to the doctrine and discipline
of that part of the Church which ordains him. That is done as a
matter of church government rather than as the profession that the
Episcopal Church is in any way the exclusive heir of the Christian
religion. Indeed, the Preface to the Ordinal makes it clear that
clergy of other religious bodies may be recognized and received
into our ministry if they have had confirmation and ordination by
a bishop of the universal Church.

We have seen in an earlier chapter that the American Episcopal
Church is but one part of the Anglican Communion, composed of
churches throughout the world in full communion with the See
of Canterbury. We have seen further that the Anglican Communion itself is only a part of the universal Catholic Church.
Like the Roman Catholics and the Eastern Orthodox Christians, we
hold that the Church is to be found wherever there is a loyal body
of Christians holding the Catholic faith and governed by a bishop
in apostolic succession.

The term *Apostolic Succession* has frequently been misunder-
stood and has often been the subject of controversy between various
bodies of Christians. The best Anglican definition of Apostolic
Succession is to be found in the Preface to the Ordinal in the Book
of Common Prayer:

It is evident unto all men, diligently reading Holy Scripture and ancient
Authors, that from the Apostles' time there have been these Orders of
Ministers in Christ's Church,—Bishops, Priests, and Deacons. Which
Offices were evermore had in such reverend estimation that no man
might presume to execute any of them, except he were first called, tried,
examined and known to have such qualities as are requisite for the
same; and also by public Prayer, with Imposition of Hands, were approved and admitted thereunto by lawful Authority. And therefore to
the intent that these Orders may be continued, and reverently used and

esteemed in this Church, no man shall be accounted or taken to be a lawful Bishop, Priest, or Deacon, in this Church, or suffered to execute any of the said Functions, except he be called, tried, examined, and admitted thereunto, according to the Form hereafter following, or hath had Episcopal Consecration or Ordination.

Critics of the Church have sometimes referred scornfully to the doctrine of Apostolic Succession as "the pipeline theory of the Church." They have caricatured it as a sort of plumbing system running through the ages, whereby the water of grace, poured into the Apostles, flows from them into the pipeline of the episcopate, down to the present through the faucet that happens to represent the present bishop of any given diocese. As a purely mechanical illustration it is not too far from the truth; but Apostolic Succession is something far more important and significant than a merely mechanical means of perpetuating the ministry.

There is no doubt that our Lord himself conferred upon the twelve Apostles the duty and responsibility of constituting and continuing his Church. He said to them, "Go ye therefore, and teach all nations, baptizing them in the name of the Father, and of the Son, and of the Holy Ghost; teaching them to observe all things whatsoever I have commanded you: and lo I am with you alway, even unto the end of the earth" (Matt. 28:19,20). Moreover he invested them with the authority of reconciliation: "Whose soever sins ye remit, they are remitted unto them; and whose soever sins ye retain, they are retained" (John 20:23). Furthermore, he laid upon them the duty of constant celebration of the Holy Communion: "This do ye, as oft as ye drink it, in remembrance of me" (I Cor. 11:25).

So important did the Apostles regard their duties that their first act after Pentecost was to choose a new apostle to fill the vacancy left by the defection and suicide of Judas. They cast lots and chose St. Matthias to fill out their number and to have all the powers of the apostolic ministry. Subsequently, they recognized St. Paul as having been called in a particular way to the apostolate through the direct commissioning of our Lord when he appeared to him in a vision on the road to Damascus.

Tradition has it that when the Apostles scattered to carry their ministry throughout the world, each of them chose a particular area in which to exercise his apostolic oversight. St. James the Less remained in Jerusalem as its bishop; St. John went to Damascus; St. Thomas perhaps to India; St. Peter and St. Paul to the western Roman Empire; and others to various parts of the known world.

It soon became apparent that the entire ministry of the Church could not be exercised by a handful of Apostles, and as the second coming of our Lord was not to take place during their lifetime (as apparently originally anticipated), they must select assistants and successors.

Probably the earliest assistants to the Apostles were the deacons, whose appointment is recorded in the book of Acts. Their function was not to preach or to celebrate the sacraments but to handle the temporal affairs of the Church, to take up collections for the relief of needy Christians and for the financing of missionary enterprises, and to minister to the sick and to widows and orphans.

When St. Paul and other Apostles began to travel widely throughout the Roman Empire and beyond, and to establish churches in remote communities, it became necessary to appoint men to minister to these communities after the Apostle had gone on his way. Thus, St. Paul and others ordained presbyter-bishops to whom in turn they entrusted the full powers of the ministry, including the right to ordain others. In time, they were to be separated into two orders—bishops who held the full power of the ministry and right to ordain, and presbyters or priests to whom were delegated the authority to celebrate the other sacraments, to preach and to teach, but not to ordain.

Thus, at the end of the first three Christian centuries, the threefold ministry of bishops, priests, and deacons had fully emerged. Exactly how it came about cannot be fully traced because the nature of the early Church did not demand much record keeping. It is, however, quite clear that by the end of the second or beginning of the third century the threefold ministry was universal in the Christian Church. In each large center there was a bishop who exercised the powers of government and ordination; and under him a body of priests who celebrated the holy Mysteries and exercised pastoral administration, and deacons who did not perform major sacramental functions but who assisted with the temporal side of the ministry.

The threefold ministry has come down through the Church to the present day. The evidence for its orderly perpetuation is overwhelming. Such ancient sees as Jerusalem, Antioch, Rome, and subsequently Lyons, in France, and Canterbury, in England, have preserved the records of the succession of their bishops in their respective sees. Records of the actual participants in consecrations are not quite so old, although they go back into very early Christian history. It is apparent, however, that from very early days three or more bishops normally participated in the consecration of every new bishop, and thus the record of the apostolic succession is not a chain dependent upon its weakest link but rather a web of interlocking consecrations too strong to be broken by the weakness of any one strand.

Until the time of the Reformation, there was no question of the necessity of the apostolic succession. Luther and Calvin and Zwingli were the first to break the net by contending that there was but one order of the ministry and that presbyters were qualified to continue it, with or without the help of bishops. (That is the theory still held by most churches of Lutheran or Calvinist descent, although it is noteworthy that bishops in the apostolic succession have continued to have the exclusive right to ordain in Lutheran Sweden, even to the present day.)

Later arose the theory that any congregation of the faithful was able to call its own minister and to set him apart without the necessity of laying on of hands by a bishop or by a presbytery. (This is the pure Congregational tradition, although in practice modern

Congregationalists generally follow a presbyterial form of ordination.)

When the Church of England released itself from the shackles
of Rome in the sixteenth century, it definitely retained the ancient
doctrine of Apostolic Succession and rejected the "modern" notions
of Presbyterianism or Congregationalism. The record of the English
bishoprics shows that great care was taken to insure that bishops
were consecrated only by the laying on of hands of other bishops in
the apostolic succession and tradition. Thus, the Church of England,
and through it the Episcopal Church, retains with the Roman
Catholic and the Eastern Orthodox churches both the theory and
the practice of apostolic ordination and consecration, with the
historic threefold ministry of bishops, priests, and deacons.

Most Protestant bodies in western Europe and America have
lost that tradition and practice. They reject the Catholic tradition
that the bishop is the essential center of unity of the Church, and
that the episcopate collectively is the guarantor of the continuity and
apostolicity of the Church. It is not surprising, therefore, that
Anglicans have not been able to achieve intercommunion with
other religious bodies which reject the Apostolic Succession. It is an
ancient saying that "Where the bishop is, there is the Church"; and
the Anglican churches hold firmly to that indispensable element of
Catholic faith and order.

How all this works out in practice may be seen in any parish
or diocese. Almost every Confirmation class, particularly of adults,
contains two categories of aspirants or catechumens, to use the
ancient term. The larger group consists of those who have been
baptized either in the Episcopal Church or in any church that
recognizes Baptism by water "in the name of the Father, and of
the Son, and of the Holy Ghost." The other smaller group consists
of those who come from another Christian body which has the
apostolic ministry and who have already been confirmed in that
other church. If they are from one of the Eastern Orthodox bodies,
they may have been confirmed in infancy; if from the Roman

Catholic Church, they have probably been confirmed at a very early age: in either case Confirmation is not repeated in the Episcopal Church, for they are "received" into "this branch of the Catholic Church." Thus, their confirmation by a bishop in their former Church is fully recognized when they are admitted to communicant status in the Episcopal Church.

Similarly, if a priest of the Roman Catholic Church enters the ministry of the Episcopal Church, he is not "reordained" but is received as a priest on the basis of his previous ordination and, after taking the necessary vows of obedience, is authorized to act as a priest in this Church.

On the other hand, if a layman is received from another church not of the apostolic tradition, he must be confirmed before he can receive full communicant status, even though he may have undergone a ceremony of confirmation by a Lutheran minister or by the minister of some other Protestant body. Similarly, if a Protestant minister wishes to enter the priesthood of the Episcopal Church, and is found otherwise qualified, he must be confirmed and ordained deacon and priest before he is authorized to exercise the sacred ministry of the Church.

However, by a recent special provision of the Church's law (Canon 36), the bishop may read a preface to the service acknowledging the candidate as "already a minister of Christ," and may include a similar acknowledgement in his certificate of ordination, "adding to that commission the grace and authority of Holy Orders as understood and required by this Church for the exercise of the ministry."

These procedures do not mean that the Episcopal Church does not recognize that laymen in other churches are quite as fully Christians as Episcopalians are, or that ministers of churches not of the apostolic succession are not true ministers of Christ. They may indeed be very effective and devoted pastors to their people, and that is fully recognized. However, Protestant ministers do not claim to be priests of apostolic succession and, since the Episcopal

Church has carefully preserved that priesthood and intends (along with three-quarters of Christendom) to perpetuate it, they must be ordained by a bishop before they can be permitted to exercise the functions of the priesthood.

When we apply that doctrine to Christian unity, it will readily be seen that an almost insuperable problem arises when we are dealing with Protestant bodies. Most of them do not believe in the Apostolic Succession and they think that our requirement of it is somehow a reflection on their own ministry. They are not willing to be ordained by a bishop or even to undergo what might be called supplementary or conditional ordination. We, for our part, cannot accept their ministry on the same basis as our own without being disloyal to our own conviction and to "the One, Holy, Catholic, and Apostolic Church" of history.

Increasingly efforts are being made in many parts of the Christian world to bridge the gap. The first experiment was that of the Church of South India which was a union of churches of Anglican, Presbyterian, and Congregational backgrounds, and which also includes Methodists of English background. In that union it was agreed that the historic episcopate should be continued and that all ordinations after the time of union should be by bishops; however, the ministers not episcopally ordained, who came into the Church at the time of union and certain others who have gone there since as missionaries have not been ordained by bishops and so are not ministers in the apostolic succession. In other words, we recognize their bishops as true bishops and the presbyters who have been ordained by them as true priests. Similarly, we recognize the laymen who have been confirmed by a bishop as eligible to receive the Holy Communion at our altars; but we are unable to give a similar degree of recognition to their unconfirmed laymen or to their ministers not ordained by bishops. It is all very confused and shows the dangers of following theories instead of conforming to what the Church actually has done in all times and all places among all people.

On the other hand we have been able to enter into full communion with the Old Catholic Churches of Europe, the Polish National Catholic Church in America, the Philippine Independent Church, and the Episcopal churches in Spain and Portugal, since those bodies, some large, some small, have retained or regained the apostolic succession.

We also recognize, of course, Roman Catholic and Eastern Orthodox bishops and priests as ministers in the apostolic succession. There the barriers to full unity are on other grounds.

The Roman Catholic Church does not officially recognize that our ministry is composed of true bishops, priests, and deacons; although many of their scholars might be prepared to do so on the basis of their own studies. Unfortunately, they are prevented from extending such recognition by a papal encyclical issued by Pope Leo XIII in 1896 which declared Anglican Orders invalid. Happily the encyclical has never been proclaimed as an infallible pronouncement by the papacy; moreover, the infusion into the Anglican ministry of Old Catholic orders (which are recognized by Rome) may make it possible to reopen the question at some time in the not-too-distant future.

On the other hand, most of the Eastern Orthodox churches do recognize the validity of Anglican ordinations. Relations between our Church and the Eastern Orthodox are increasingly cordial and in the providence of God may, in due time, lead to some measure of intercommunion. The major difficulty is the Eastern Orthodox teaching that the Orthodox Church is the only true one, and it has so far been unable to recognize any Christians outside the Eastern Orthodox fold as members of the visible Church.

All the foregoing may have been rather technical and perhaps of little interest or concern to many of the lay people who read this book; nevertheless, these are some of the major factors that divide the Church at the present day, as they have done for many centuries.

There is, however, a new climate in the Christian world that strongly emphasizes the unity of all Christians despite the barriers which separate them into different communions, denominations, and churches. Nowhere was the freshening atmosphere more evident than in the benevolent attitude of the late Pope John XXIII in his reference to those whom he termed "our separated brethren," and in the deliberations of the Second Vatican Council.

When Pope John received an Archbishop of Canterbury for the first time since the Reformation, and later when he welcomed our own Presiding Bishop, it did not mean that he was recognizing the validity of Anglican Orders. It did mean that doors were opened that had been closed for many centuries and that once again Christian brethren were able to see each other as children of the same God and as co-workers in the building of the kingdom. Now that the doors have been opened, nobody can tell what will come out of them.

From a human and historical view, Christian unity may seem to be impossible. In the providence of God, however, all things are possible and surely the unity of Christendom for which our Lord himself prayed is not beyond the capabilities of the God who created the heavens and the earth, and who is the Father of all mankind.

O God, the Father of our Lord Jesus Christ, our only Saviour, the Prince of Peace; Give us grace seriously to lay to heart the great dangers we are in by our unhappy divisions. Take away all hatred and prejudice, and whatsoever else may hinder us from godly union and concord: that as there is but one Body and one Spirit, and one hope of our calling, one Lord, one Faith, one Baptism, one God and Father of us all, so we may be all of one heart and of one soul, united in one holy bond of truth and peace, of faith and charity, and may with one mind and one mouth glorify thee; through Jesus Christ our Lord. *Amen.*

(Prayer Book, page 37)

Ecumenical Conferences and Conversations

CHAPTER NINE

IT HAS been said that the "great new fact of our time," so far as Christianity is concerned, is the ecumenical movement—the drawing together in friendly conversations of churches long separated from one another. The growing movement, stemming from the Edinburgh missionary conference of 1910, the Lambeth appeal to all Christians in 1920, and the first World Conference on Faith and Order in 1927, is squarely based on our Lord's high priestly prayer, "that they all may be one; as thou, Father, art in me, and I in thee, that they also may be one in us: that the world may believe that thou hast sent me" (John 17:21).

Barbara Ward, writing on "The Quest for Christian Unity" in the *Atlantic Monthly* (August, 1962), noted that the short-term prospects for Christian unity "look somewhat meager." On the long-term basis, however, she adds:

It took nearly forty years to bring the World Council into being. Its discussions with the Orthodox and [Roman] Catholic communions may take as many more. It is in this longer perspective that there are grounds for believing that the movement toward Christian unity is gathering and will continue to gather enough strength to bring the major communions into a single Christian Church. . . . The men who meet in the ecumenical encounter are all Christians. They believe in a God who is gracious to those who seek His truth and who sends His spirit of understanding to hearts and minds genuinely desiring to fulfill His will. That God's will *is* a reunited Church is the essential premise of the ecumenical movement. Can any believer really hold that the earnest prayer of so many dedicated Christians will not one day be answered? That the love and wisdom needed for reunion will not inspire men and women who so urgently seek it?

My own experience in the ecumenical movement covers nearly forty years. In that time I have seen it grow from the fad of the few to the concern of many, including the officials of the historic churches. My father was a delegate from the Episcopal Church to the first World Conference on Faith and Order in 1927. As a fledgling editor just out of college, I received and published his dispatches from that meeting, and began to absorb something of his enthusiasm for the reunion of Christendom. Upon his death in 1932, I was appointed to the continuation committee and attended my first meeting in Denmark in 1935. There I met such pioneers of the ecumenical movement as William Temple (then Archbishop of York, later of Canterbury); G. K. A. Bell, Bishop of Chichester; Bishop Irenaeus of Serbia; Archbishop Germanos, Metropolitan of the Greek Orthodox Church; Professor Adolf Deissmann of Germany; Professor Nicholas Arseniev of Russia, Canon Leonard Hodgson and Dr. R. Newton Flew of England; Bishop Brilioth of Sweden; Dr. John H. MacCracken, William Adams Brown, and Dean W. L. Sperry of the United States; and others whose names are famous in interdenominational annals.

In editorial correspondence to *The Living Church* (August 31, 1935), of which I was then editor, I wrote:

Humanly speaking, the reconciliation of the great difficulties that stand in the way of a united world-wide Christian Church seems to be, and is, impossible. Even the reunion of Protestantism, to say nothing of intercommunion between a united Protestantism on the one hand and united Anglicanism, Orthodoxy, and Old Catholicism on the other, seems an insurmountable task, while the inclusion of the great Roman Catholic communion in any program of unity appears so visionary as scarcely to be worthy of serious consideration. Yet what is humanly impossible is wholly feasible in the providence of Almighty God, to whom all things are possible; and the believer in our blessed Lord cannot fail to have confidence that in due time and under the guidance of the Holy Spirit His great prayer, that we may all be one—that there may be one fold and one Shepherd—must finally be realized. . . . Perhaps it will require a miracle to achieve the goal of Christian unity. Indeed it would certainly seem that that is the case. But as Catholic Christians we believe in miracles, and we know of no article of faith that puts a time limit to the accomplishments of them. Indeed our Lord, commenting on His own miracles, told His disciples that they should perform even greater ones in His name. If God requires of us a miracle for the attainment of that for which He prayed, then He will also make it possible for that miracle to be performed. For our part, we must prepare for it by expecting it, by watching and praying for it, and by implementing our prayers with our deeds and our lives. Thus, when in the divine wisdom the time is accomplished—whether it be soon or late, gradual or sudden, we shall be ready.

Today, nearly thirty years later, I could not improve upon this statement; indeed I would be prepared to say that in the new climate of ecumenical relations the miracle has already begun.

Since then I have attended many international and interdenominational councils, conferences, and conversations, including the second World Conference on Faith and Order in Edinburgh, 1937, the third one, Lund, Sweden, 1952; the first Assembly of the World Council of Churches at Amsterdam, 1948, the second, Evanston, Illinois, 1953; the third, New Delhi, India, 1961; and innumerable sessions of continuation committees, commissions, study groups, conferences, and the extensive panoply of meetings that make up the process of the ecumenical movement.

Some of them were stimulating and fruitful, others were dull beyond belief. There were times when it seemed that we were playing old records over and over again, times when the participants actually seemed to be headed backward. I have listened to interminable German theological papers, invariably going back to creation regardless of the purported subject, to scintillating French speeches, cultivated English addresses, and impatient American demands for action. I have listened on earphones to the English translations of foreign theological essays (and found in Amersterdam, to my delight, that by turning the dial I could receive the BBC broadcasts instead!); I have listened to the monotonous reading of papers with the printed text before me; I have plowed through inadequate English translations of ponderous German or Scandinavian discourses; and—on rare occasions—I have heard and understood the ringing challenges of a Temple, a Ramsey, a Tillich, or a Stanley Jones.

For many years I was virtually the only layman adrift in a sea of theological barques. Perhaps it was not a bad thing, for occasionally, especially in smaller conferences or committee meetings, I was able to say a word or write a paragraph in a draft document that would bring the discussion out of the realm of speculative theology and into "a language understood of the people." More recently, increasingly since the 1953 Evanston meeting, the voice of the layman has been more frequently heard, and the level of discussion has gradually become more intelligible to the man and woman in the pew. That is all to the good; indeed, it is essential if the ecumenical movement is really to begin to move and to acquire momentum at what the cliché mongers are accustomed to term "the grass-roots level."

Simultaneously with what may be called the conciliar approach to Christian unity, there have been a number of successful conversations and negotiations between two churches or among groups of similar churches, looking toward church unity or reunion. In the United States the union of Congregational and Evangelical Reformed churches resulted in the United Church of Christ; the union of the northern and southern branches of the Methodist Episcopal Church brought about one body named the Methodist Church (but left most Negro Methodists in segregated churches); various Presbyterian branches united to form the United Presbyterian Church of the U.S.A., and the joining of some of the Lutheran synods made the Lutheran Church of America.

The Episcopal Church has also engaged in conversations and negotiations, in some of which I have shared as a member of the Commission on Approaches to Unity and later as a member of the

Commission on Ecumenical Relations. In the 1930's I was a member of our commission which negotiated with the Presbyterians—a minority member as it turned out after the development of the unsatisfactory basis of union which led to rejection of the plan and termination of the conversations at the General Convention of 1946. I had the privilege of presenting to the House of Deputies, in 1960, the resolution which resulted in the concordat with the Polish National Catholic Church as a part of the larger intercommunion between the Anglican and Old Catholic churches. I had a share in drafting the report that resulted in similar agreements with the Spanish Episcopal Reformed Church and the (Portuguese) Lusitanian Church. I had also the great pleasure of presiding over the House of Deputies when it ratified the agreement of full communion with the Philippine Independent Church in 1961, and subsequently of serving on the joint advisory council of the Episcopal and Independent churches in the Philippines. It is significant, I think, that of all the discussions and negotiations held by the Episcopal Church so far, the only ones that have had a successful outcome have been those with churches of Catholic faith and episcopal polity. Our Church proudly claims to be both Protestant and Catholic, and with that claim I fully agree; but when all the talking is over, it is with the Catholic churches that we are able to come to full agreement and full communion.

There is one area, however, in which Anglican and Protestant churches have been able to achieve some degree of unity: the Church of South India. Four dioceses of the Church of India, Pakistan, Burma, and Ceylon, deriving from the Church of England, in 1947 broke off from the Anglican communion (with the blessing of the Lambeth Conference), and united with the churches of Congregational, Presbyterian, and Wesleyan Methodist origin to form an indigenous and self-governing Church that was intended to embrace all non-Roman and non-Orthodox Christians in southern India. It was and continues to be so far the most successful union across the normal Catholic-Protestant, or Episcopal-Congregational lines. It did, however, sever the unity of Anglicanism in that part of the world, and that unity has never been fully restored.

I was one of five members of a special committee sent to India in 1954 to study the Church of South India, and to report whether intercommunion between it and the Episcopal Church could be established and how. Our mission was only partially successful. We (Bishops Binsted and Lichtenberger, the Rev. Drs. Gardiner M. Day and John Butler, and myself) returned with great enthusiasm for the new Church and with the conviction that it was moving toward increasing inner unity on a Catholic basis. As a result of our report and of the report of a theological committee, the General Convention recognized a sort of partial intercommunion, whereby the bishops of the Church of South India and those priests who had been episcopally ordained before or after the union, were permitted to celebrate the Holy Communion in Episcopal churches, provided that they did not also celebrate in non-Episcopal churches in the same community; and whereby confirmed members of the Church of South India could receive Holy Communion in Episcopal churches. It was, however, a unilateral action on the part of the Episcopal Church, and it did not prove satisfactory to the Church of South India; consequently it has been of little practical effect.

The experiment of church union in South India has taught us many things. On the positive side, it has shown us that churches of Catholic and Protestant traditions can form a viable union and that, with sound leadership on the part of bishops, other clergy, and laymen, it can develop and grow in a Catholic direction. On the negative side, it has shown us that a Church in which the problem of the ministry is not solved at the outset will continue to be handicapped, especially in its relations with churches that hold firmly to Apostolic Succession and the historic threefold ministry. On the rock of that still unsolved problem, similar proposed unions of churches in northern India, Pakistan, and Ceylon have foundered or, at least, been temporarily grounded.

A current approach toward the solution of the matter, and the anticipated establishment of a church united across the Catholic-Protestant barrier, is the Consultation on Church Union now in progress among representatives of the Episcopal, United Presbyterian, and Methodist churches, together with the United Church of Christ and certain related bodies in this country. It is too early to say how the conversations will develop, or whether they will lead to actual negotiations and a plan of church union. The object, in the words of the Rev. Eugene Carson Blake in his famous sermon at Grace Cathedral, San Francisco, is to form a church that shall be "truly Catholic, truly Evangelical, and truly Reformed."

It would be easy for an Episcopalian to retort (and some have done so) that we already belong to a church that is truly Catholic, truly Reformed, and truly Evangelical. (Many Presbyterians, Methodists, and Congregationalists might claim the same.) The truth is, however, that we are not so Catholic as we might be, not so reformed as we could be, and not so evangelical as we should be—and the same is true of the other churches in the consultation. The hopeful part of the approach is that it seeks Christian unity on the basis of the maximum that each participating body can contribute to it, not the minimum set of vague formularies to which the least objection can be found. It is devoutly to be hoped that the concept of maximum contribution to unity will continue to guide the consultants and the churches that they represent, and that, under the guidance of the Holy Spirit, this may lead to a solution of problems that have hitherto proved insoluble. At this point, however, it looks like a long, slow process; and those who confidently predict that it will lead to an acceptable plan of union within two or ten or even twenty years are, I fear, doomed to disappointment.

So far as the Episcopal Church is concerned, we are committed to move slowly and in concert with the other churches of the Anglican Communion. The Anglican Congress of 1963 demonstrated anew the strength of the bonds which bind us to the mother Church of England and to our sister Anglican churches throughout the world. We must do nothing that would jeopardize that very real and world-wide unity which already exists, or break the communion that we have achieved with other churches that have come to be known (rather ineptly) as the "Wider Episcopal Fellowship." Nor should we move in the direction of Protestant unity at the expense of our increasingly close relationship with the churches of the Eastern Orthodox Communion, and of the new and exciting prospect of a better understanding and fellowship with the Roman Catholic Church.

The recent entry of the Roman Catholic Church into the ecumenical dialogue is perhaps the most thrilling episode in the rapidly developing story of interchurch relationships. The door between the Roman Catholic Church and the Anglican, Orthodox, and Protestant churches, closed and bolted four hundred years, has at last been unlocked, and even opened a little bit. There are signs that under Pope Paul VI, following in the footsteps of the lovable John XXIII, it may be opened wider, leading to increasingly close relationships and better understanding between those Christians who dwell in the many mansions on either side of it.

Here it may be well to note that the door was unbolted on the Anglican and Protestant side some decades ago. The 1920 Lambeth Appeal to All Christian People specifically included the Roman Catholic Church in its invitation.

The resolution sponsored by Dr. Manning and Bishop Brent in the 1910 General Convention asked that "all Christian communions throughout the world which confess our Lord Jesus Christ as God and Saviour be asked to unite with us in arranging for and conducting . . . a conference"; and the 1920 Lambeth Appeal was also addressed to "all Christian people." The original appeal was sent (in Latin) to all the cardinals and bishops of the Roman Catholic Church. In 1919 a delegation presented the proposal in person to Pope Benedict XV; and although the holy father was cordial in his conversation with the delegates, they were handed on leaving the following official statement:

The Holy Father, after having thanked them for their visit, stated that as successor of St. Peter and Vicar of Christ he had no greater desire than that there should be one fold and one Shepherd. His Holiness added that the teaching and practice of the Roman Catholic Church regarding the unity of the visible Church of Christ was well known to everybody and that therefore it would not be possible for the Catholic Church to take part in such a congress as the one proposed. His Holiness, however, by no means wishes to disapprove of the congress in question for those who are not in union with the Chair of Peter; on the contrary, he earnestly desires and prays that, if the congress is practicable, those who take part in it may, by the grace of God, see the light and become reunited to the visible Head of the Church, by whom they will be received with open arms.[1]

This statement, needless to say, precluded any official participation of the Roman Catholic Church in world conferences for many years to come, though the invitation was never withdrawn by the continuation committees or the subsequent organization of the World Council of Churches.

It is only fair to note, however, that despite the apparent finality of the Church of Rome's refusal to participate in the Faith and Order movement, it has shown a lively interest in the development of the ecumenical movement among Anglicans, Orthodox, and Protestants almost from the outset, and particularly since the formation of the World Council of Churches in 1948. At most of the major sessions of the World Council, and at the Faith and Order Conferences, Roman Catholic journalists and theologians have been present, first as accredited press representatives and later as unofficial observers. More recently, beginning at the preparatory meetings at St. Andrews, Scotland, in 1960, and notably at the New Delhi Assembly in 1961, the Vatican has sent some of its ablest theologians as official observers, and the Roman Catholic press has had comprehensive and sympathetic reports. Moreover, some of the most penetrating and constructive criticisms of the ecumenical movement have been written by Roman Catholic observers and scholars.

In 1960 occurred an event of great promise to the entire Christian world, and one of special significance for Anglicans. Lord Fisher of Lambeth, then Archbishop of Canterbury, made a courtesy call on Pope John XXIII—the first time that an Archbishop of Canterbury had talked with a pope since the Reformation. In 1961, on his way to the New Delhi Assembly, the Right Rev. Arthur Lichtenberger, Presiding Bishop of the Episcopal Church, made a similar visit to the Pope; and many other dignitaries—Anglican, Eastern Orthodox, and Protestant—have done likewise since then.

I was glad to accompany Bishop Lichtenberger on his historic 1961 visit, along with the Rt. Rev. Lauriston Scaife, Bishop of Western New York, the Rev. Canon Bernard C. Pawley, of Ely Cathedral, and the Rev. Wilbur C. Woodhams, Rector of St. Paul's American Episcopal Church in Rome. Following a private conversation with the Presiding Bishop, the Pope received the rest of us most graciously, chatted informally, and expressed his personal interest in the assembly that was about to be held. He also spoke of the Second Vatican Council, which he had recently called, and his pleasure that the non-Roman churches would be represented there by delegate-observers. We presented His Holiness with a beautifully bound copy of the Book of Common Prayer, and he thanked us for it, saying that he was often wakeful at night and that he would keep it at his bedside to read his devotions from it at such times. In return, he gave us medals, saying modestly he hoped we would not mind that they bore his profile, but that by papal custom all medals were so designed. Needless to say, we not only did not mind but were very happy to receive these tokens of his affection for us, who were fellow Christians although of another room in the household of the faithful.

It was because of his very warm and genuine Christian love embracing all mankind, which was so frequently and simply expressed by John XXIII, that the whole world mourned his death in 1963. He was a great and saintly Christian; and he it was who unbolted the door and opened it to the free discussion and mutual trust that may, in God's good time, lead to the healing of the centuries-old breach between Rome and separated Christian communions.

It is too soon to write of the Second Vatican Council and of its possible development of closer relations with the World Council and with the churches that make up its membership, except to say that Pope Paul VI has not only carried on the great work begun by his predecessor but also has encouraged the council to move forward in its work of internal Church renewal, as well as strengthening the ties with other Christian churches. On the very day after his coronation, he called together such of the delegate-observers as were in Rome at the time, and assured them of his cordiality toward the "separated brethren." In a moving account of that audience, the Rev. Wilbur C. Woodhams wrote:

We were warmly greeted, the bishops with a hand-shake as brothers, we priests took his hand and "bent the knee" as is proper to a bishop. Then we sat in a semi-circle with the Pope in the middle on his slightly higher chair. He spoke to us in English, then switched to Italian, in which he is more comfortable. The atmosphere was a relaxed one of Christian understanding—we might have been gathered around our own bishop at home to talk about local missionary strategy. . . . The Pope spoke to us simply and directly about his own thankfulness for the new understanding in the Church, and his intention to continue. My impression is that he has already gone beyond his predecessor, which he is able to do because of what happened in the time of Pius XII and John XXIII. He was most open in asking that other parts of the Church present to the Church of Rome questions which they feel Rome must answer if the Church is to be healed. . . .

After his words, the Pope asked if we would like to respond, and the Bishop of Ripon said, "Thank you." The door is open and our response and initiative will have to come with great prayer and thought. Then happened something of which none of us could have dreamed a few years ago, yet must always be in the mind of God. His Holiness suggested that we say the Lord's Prayer together, each in his own tongue—and so we did, standing close together in that magnificent red room as if we were what we are, sinful men being filled by the Holy Ghost, primitive Christians of what must always be the "early Church." Then, not offering us his lordly blessing, Paul VI gave each of us in turn the kiss of peace—his hands on our shoulders and ours on his, as Christian brothers always have.[2]

May God grant that the Christian world, both Roman and non-Roman, will respond thoughtfully and prayerfully, and in the same spirit of Christian brotherhood, to that gracious invitation to fellowship and fruitful conversation! The road ahead will be a long and still one, beset with many pitfalls, but as an ancient proverb says, even the longest journey must begin with a single step. Our Lord pointed the way two thousand years ago when he prayed "that they all may be one . . . that the world may believe."

The Anglican Communion and Mission

CHAPTER TEN

IT IS not surprising that while the Episcopal Church claims to be both Catholic and Protestant, so far all "completed action" in the field of Christian unity has been with churches of the Catholic tradition. For my part, although I value many of the elements of Protestantism, I regard myself as a Catholic first and only secondly as an Episcopalian. I am an Episcopalian because I firmly believe that the Episcopal Church is not only a Catholic Church but represents the truest form of the Catholic faith for Christians of the Western tradition. Protestantism tends to subtract some elements from the Catholic faith or to emphasize certain doctrines at the expense of others. Roman Catholicism, on the other hand, adds to the faith such dogmas as the Immaculate Conception, the Assumption of the Blessed Virgin Mary, and the infallibility of the Pope. These beliefs are not to be found in the Holy Scriptures or in the teaching of the early Church Fathers. I hope and pray that Anglicanism may never lose its grip upon the primitive faith and order of the undivided Catholic Church. If it did, it would cease to be a part of the Church built upon the faith of the apostles, our Lord himself being the cornerstone.

Closely related to Christian unity is the universal mission of the Church. No Church can truly be the Church if it tries to keep its faith to itself and its own members: it is a paradox of the Christian faith that one can only keep it by giving it away—and that is true both of individuals and of corporate Christianity.

With these things in mind, let's look at the Anglican Communion in the light of its own mission to the world. The Anglican Communion is unique in the Christian world. It consists of some forty-two million baptized members grouped in eighteen national churches, bound together by a common ministry and sacraments, despite the most diverse differences of nationality and race. One of the great unifying factors is the Book of Common Prayer; yet most of the churches have their own Prayer Books, differing in detail but alike in their essentials: thus you and I can be just as much at home in an Anglican church in London, Australia, Borneo, or Japan as we would in New York, Chicago, or San Francisco.

The largest Anglican Church is, of course, the Church of England, which claims a membership of twenty-seven million baptized persons. Perhaps only three to five million of them are active Churchmen, but to their number must be added another two million in Scotland, Ireland, and Wales, bringing the effective strength of Anglicanism in the British Isles to about seven million members.

It may surprise you, as it did me, to learn that the second largest Anglican Church is the Church of England in Australia, which has 3,500,000 baptized members. In the same part of the world, but separately constituted, is the church of the province of New Zealand which has an additional 760,000 members, thus bringing the Anglican churches "down under" close to 5,000,000 members.

The third largest Anglican Church is our own Episcopal Church with 3,345,000 members. It is interesting to note, however, that in the five self-governing provinces in Africa there are more than 3,500,000 Anglicans. Does it surprise you to learn that there are more African than American members of the Anglican communion?

Despite its great geographical, national, and racial spread there is an inner unity to the Anglican Communion, which is often unrecognized. The Rev. Canon Howard Johnson, of the Cathedral Church of St. John the Divine, New York City, points out, for example, how surprised were English Christians in Argentina when he told them that his next stop was Brazil. "Surely," they exclaimed, "there are no Anglicans in Brazil!" They were astounded when he told them that Brazil has three missionary districts with a total of some thirty-one thousand Episcopalians.

All overseas Anglicans or Episcopalians are products of missionary effort from the home churches in Britain, United States, Canada, and Australia. There is, however, a significant difference in the missionary approach of the British churches and that of the American Church. British missionary expansion has traditionally been due to the work of societies such as the Society for Promoting the Gospel and the Church Missionary Society—the former of which, incidentally, was responsible for missionary work in American colonial days. In our own Church, however, overseas missions are the responsibility of the General Convention and its agency the National Council, and therefore the concern of each individual member of the Church.

There are advantages and disadvantages in both English and American methods, as there are differences in the aim "or objective" of the British and American churches. Under the British system, overseas dioceses are grouped into provinces as soon as possible and become self-governing churches while still receiving aid from the mother church. In the American system, the overseas missions remain a part of the home church. Their bishops are members of the American House of Bishops and they send deputies to the General Convention in the United States. Their missionaries are appointed by the National Council, and they are fully responsible to the National Council for their programs and budgets. They remain "missionary districts" of the American Church.

The American system also has grave disadvantages. One of them is that it tends toward ecclesiastical colonialism and makes the overseas churches almost entirely dependent upon the Church at home. Even if there is a native bishop, as is increasingly the case, he has to submit all of his important policy decisions to the Overseas Department of the National Council in New York, and the whole process of nationalization of the Church is slowed down, to say nothing of restricting the episcopacy. With the strong feeling of nationalization throughout the world, this system can be, and often is, a source of considerable irritation.

The American system also means in practice that it is virtually impossible for the Church in another nation to become self-governing. The only exceptions under our system were the churches in Japan and China, where independence was forced upon them by political considerations. We have, of course, virtually lost contact with the Anglican Church in China under the Communist regime, but we have very close relationships with the Church in Japan, and make no attempt to dictate the policies of the Japanese House of Bishops. Surely, the exception is more in accordance with Anglican traditions! We really need to find some way of harmonizing the two systems of missionary administration and, at the same time, of preserving the best features of each.

We like to think that our American missionary work is effective, and we constantly receive glowing reports of it in the church press and through publications issuing from the National Council. Certainly most of our missionaries overseas are doing a remarkable job, sometimes under great difficulties, and we honor them for it. Nevertheless, it is a fact that after more than one hundred years of missionary endeavor the Episcopal Church today has only some 250,000 baptized members outside the United States! We have established no provinces or national churches (with the two exceptions I have noted), and all of our overseas missionary districts are directly dependent upon the General Convention and the National Council.

By way of contrast, the Anglican Church of West Africa, evangelized from England, has 750,000 baptized members organized as a self-governing province; but right in the midst of it is our missionary district in Liberia with 9,600 members, entirely oriented toward the United States! The two bishops in Liberia are not members of the West African House of Bishops, but have to make the long journey back to the United States to attend meetings of our House of Bishops. The Liberian Churchmen are Anglicans just as much as those of Ghana and the other adjoining countries. Why should they be separated from them in an artificial way?

Again, the Anglican Church of the West Indies is organized into a province with eight dioceses and 980,000 members. In the same area the American Episcopal Church has five missionary districts with 125,000 members, all tied to the American Church. Four of the five missionary districts, in fact, belong not to the province of the West Indies but to the province of New York and New Jersey!

Look at Brazil where the work of the Church covers enormous areas and offers great opportunity for growth. There we have only thirty-one thousand members, organized into three districts of the American Church. Soon there is likely to be a fourth missionary district—but still all of the bishops and deputies have to come to the United States for their General Convention; in fact their bishops are elected by the American House of Bishops. Why shouldn't the Brazilian Church be made a truly national church with its own Houses of Bishops and of Deputies and given control over its own affairs? How would we have liked it if our own program and budgets were determined in England—or Brazil?

South America is a missionary field of importance and the Church is doing relatively little in that great continent. The National Council of our Church is, however, making a survey of the field and is likely to recommend a considerable expansion of the work, as the Anglican Congress has already done. It may be our last chance in South America which, although nominally Roman Catholic, is largely non-Christian, and where Communism is making great inroads.

One of our most successful missionary fields is the Philippine Islands. I can speak of it with some knowledge because I made a trip to the Philippines in 1963 and visited many parishes and missions of our own Church and of the Philippine Independent Church. In those strategic islands we have forty-eight thousand Episcopalians in one missionary district, with an American bishop and two Filipino suffragan bishops, still fully tied to the United States. Our Church in the Philippines alone is larger than the Church in Japan, which has ten dioceses and its own Presiding Bishop and is self-governing. Beyond that, we now have the closest kind of relationship with the Philippine Independent Church, with more than two million baptized persons, organized in about twenty dioceses and with a fully self-governing organization.

Surely, that is the basis for a national Church of the Philippines, fully self-governing and incorporating both the work of the Philippine Episcopal Church and the Philippine Independent Church. Moreover, it would be the largest non-Roman Church in the Orient and a strong bastion of freedom in that troubled part of the world.

Making these churches self-governing would not mean, of course, that they would no longer need financial help from the Church at home. Indeed, they would for many years need a great deal of assistance, both financial and missionary; but they would be truly national churches and the missionaries would serve under national bishops in a Church that was free to determine its own program and policies. I venture to suggest that it would mean a great increase in strength almost immediately; for this has proved to be the case in many other churches where the apron strings to the home Church have been cut and the primary responsibility left to national leadership.

Many of the same considerations apply to the Church at home. We still have nine continental missionary districts, plus those of Alaska and Honolulu. Is such distinction between a missionary district and a diocese still valid? A missionary district differs from a diocese in that its bishop is elected by the House of Bishops rather than by its own representatives, and it receives a varying amount of financial aid from the Home Department of the National Council. It also has reduced representation in the House of Deputies—one clerical and one lay deputy instead of the four clerical and four lay deputies to which a diocese is entitled. A so-called missionary district is in effect nothing more than a second-class partner in the work of the Church. Furthermore subsidized areas of the Church often remain so only because they have not been encouraged or made to stand on their own feet.

It may be a number of years before some of our missionary districts can become fully self-supporting, although many of them are close to it if their contributions to the program of the general Church are taken into consideration. As a matter of fact, some aided dioceses receive more help from the National Council than do some missionary districts! Usually it is for special work—work among the Indians, for example. Nevertheless, the difference between an aided diocese and a missionary district is fast becoming an artificial one. Would not the work in such areas improve if the artificial distinction were removed? It seems to me that the time has come when every jurisdiction of the Episcopal Church in the United States should be given the status of a diocese with the responsibility for electing its own bishop and with full representation in the House of Deputies. Each should, of course, also become self-supporting as soon as possible; but its first-class status as a diocese would no longer be dependent upon its ability to carry on its work unaided. The Church is one and we are members one of another.

Nothing that I have said should be construed to mean that we should curtail our gifts to missionary areas of the Church at home or abroad. Indeed, the record of the Episcopal Church in missionary support is pathetic. Our per capita giving for missions is far below that of most of our Protestant or Roman Catholic brethren, and the result is that our rate of growth in this country is barely keeping up with the population, while millions of Americans have no church affiliation.

In 1860 our ratio of communicants to the population of the country was 1 to 209. In 1940 it had become 1 to 92—a huge percentage growth in eighty years; but in the twenty years from 1940 to 1960 the ratio increased to only 1 in 86, and it is questionable if we are maintaining that ratio today.

Must we conclude that the Episcopal Church is not really a missionary church? If so, it means that we are falling down on the great commission that was given to us by our Lord himself. Moreover, we are not living up to our bounden duty as set forth in the Prayer Book—to work and pray and give for the spread of Christ's great kingdom. Do we really believe we have that duty? Do we really fullfil it to the best of our ability?

The Pentecostals and other groups of Christians, whom we are likely to call sects and to look down upon, far outstrip us in missionary zeal. Will their type of religion be the Christianity of the future?

In many parts of the world there is a great revival of Buddhism and Hinduism. The Archbishop of York at the World Council Assembly in New Delhi made a speech that shocked many of us who heard him. Christianity was growing in the world, he said, but not nearly in proportion to the growth of population and to the spread of some non-Christian religions. Today Christians are a smaller percentage of the world population than they were fifty years ago! Buddhists and Hindus, at least, believe in some kind of religion and moral values. Unfortunately, Communists who believe in neither are also growing at a rapid pace, especially in Africa and Latin America. Are we willing to leave the shape of the future to them?

The outcome will be determined by deeds, not words. Every Christian is by virtue of his Baptism a missionary, a soldier of Christ. Unfortunately, too many of us are "officer-club" soldiers, content to dillydally around in our own parish churches, to be concerned only with the music and the altar furnishings and the stained glass windows, rather than with the increasingly pagan world around us.

At the time of his visit to this country in 1961, Bishop De Mel, then of Ceylon, now Metropolitan of India, said: "It is not a fear of Communism, of other religions, or of nationalism that concerns me. We have an answer to these. What scares me is the nominal Christian. The nominal Christian betrays the Church."

Nominal Christians, uncommitted Christians, self-satisfied Christians, are not going to win the world for Christ. We need a revival of the fervent zeal that spread Christianity throughout the Roman Empire during the first three centuries of the Christian era, when to be a Christian was to risk one's very life. That is the only kind of Christianity that can survive, or that deserves to survive, in a world threatened with a paganism worse than that of the Roman Empire and with the new threat of self-destruction.

I hope that we shall do some earnest and deep rethinking of these subjects, not only at Anglican congresses and Lambeth conferences and general conventions, but in every parish church throughout the land. We must learn anew what it means to work, to give, and to pray for the spread of Christ's kingdom.

The Episcopal Church makes great claims for itself. We glory in the fact that we are a part of "the One, Holy, Catholic, Apostolic Church." We take pride in our Apostolic Succession and in the dignified and orderly services of the Book of Common Prayer. It is right that we should do so because they are all treasures committed to us not just for ourselves but for the whole Christian world. We are, however, in danger of the great sin of spiritual pride if we hold aloof from other Christians and from our communities, and rest content in our traditions. We hold them in trust and we must be prepared to share them with our Christian brethren.

Yes, and we must be prepared to learn from other Christians who also have treasures committed to their keeping. The ecumenical movement is not a one-way street nor even a two-way street; it is a great plaza in which Christians of every name and background meet to learn from one another, to give and to receive, to pray and worship and work together for the spread of Christ's kingdom throughout the world.

I believe fervently in the Episcopal Church. It is my spiritual home, the place in which I find God and try to live by his commandments. But when I stand in church with my fellow Episcopalians and recite the Creed, I do not proclaim my faith in the Episcopal Church, but in "the One, Holy, Catholic, Apostolic Church," of which the Episcopal Church is only a small part. It is to that universal Church, the very Body of Christ, to which our ultimate allegiance must be given.

O God, who has made of one blood all nations of men for to dwell on the face of the whole earth, and didst send thy blessed Son to preach peace to them that are far off and to them that are nigh; Grant that all men everywhere may seek after thee and find thee. Bring the nations into thy fold, pour out thy Spirit upon all flesh, and hasten thy kingdom; through the same thy Son Jesus Christ our Lord. *Amen.*

(Prayer Book, page 38)

The Christian Family

CHAPTER ELEVEN

SOCIOLOGISTS are agreed that the family is the basic unit of society; the Church would go further and say that the Christian family is the basic unit of Christianity. The Bible goes still further and attributes the family to the plan of God. "God setteth the solitary in families," sang the psalmist; or, in the Prayer Book version, "He is the God that maketh men to be of one mind in an house" (Ps. 68:6). St. Paul likens the Christian Church to the family: "For this cause I bow my knees unto the Father of our Lord Jesus Christ, of whom the whole family in heaven and earth is named" (Eph. 3:14-15).

Until a few generations ago the Christian family was easily identifiable. The children were baptized in infancy, and as soon as they were old enough they attended church (or Sunday school); the parents were regularly in church on Sundays; grace at meals and often family prayer at bedtime were customary. The parish priest was a regular caller, and family birthdays and anniversaries were remembered. Above all, the family stayed in one place; it was a permanent part of the community and of the parish church. When a member of the family died, his body was laid to rest in the local cemetery, which was sometimes the churchyard, and other headstones indicated that generations of the same family had been so buried.

Today all that has changed. Americans are a nomadic people —always on the move. Few people live in the community in which they were born; few children attend school in the same town from the first grade through high school; meals are likely to be movable feasts, and bedtime is irregular, varying with every member of the family and, like railroad timetables, "subject to change without notice."

A college chaplain and the rector of a suburban parish were comparing notes. "I have only four years to deal with my parishioners," lamented the chaplain. "I wish I could count on four years with the families of my congregation," exclaimed the rector.

The Christian family begins with the marriage of a Christian man and woman. It is, in the words of the Prayer Book, "an honourable estate, instituted of God, signifying unto us the mystical union that is betwixt Christ and his Church." Incidentally, and lest we forget, a civil marriage is just as binding (and just as sacramental) as a Church marriage. The part of the Church is to recognize and register the marriage, to bless it, and to pray that the husband and wife, "living faithfully together, may surely perform and keep the vow and covenant betwixt them made, . . . and may ever remain in perfect love and peace together, and live according to [God's] laws."

The nature of the "vow and covenant" is made quite explicit by the "troth" (or "truth," that is, a solemn pledge) made by each to the other: "I *John* take thee *Mary* to my wedded Wife, to have and to hold from this day forward, for better for worse, for richer for poorer, in sickness and in health, to love and to cherish, till death us do part, according to God's holy ordinance." Only after the exchange of the solemn pledge does the priest bless the ring, as a symbol of a new relationship that is never ending, and the groom place it on the bride's finger saying: "With this Ring I thee wed: In the Name of the Father, and of the Son, and of the Holy Ghost. Amen."

There is nothing transient, tentative, or temporary about the solemn vows and ceremony. Marriage is a "holy estate" into which the two persons enter "reverently, discreetly, advisedly, soberly [i.e. 'seriously-minded], and in the fear of God." The wording of the marriage service may be quaint and archaic, but its meaning is definite and clear. There is no escape clause, no provision for second thought, no suggestion that if the going gets tough the couple may be divorced, and the parties left free to enter into a new marriage relationship; only *death* can dissolve the marriage. The Church's teaching is quite clear: marriage is for life, and there is no getting around the fact. Those who do not intend a lifetime union have no business asking the Church to bless their marriage.

There is, however, the matter of so-called *hard cases*. It is an axiom that hard cases make bad law. Divorce and remarriage have become so common in our society that we tend to think of them as normal, when in fact they are highly abnormal, no matter how prevalent the custom may be. Our Lord was quite clear about this matter: "Have ye not read, that he which made them at the beginning made them male and female, and said, For this cause shall a man leave father and mother, and shall cleave to his wife: and they twain shall be one flesh? Wherefore they are no more twain, but one flesh. What therefore God hath joined together, let not man put asunder" (Matt. 19:4-6).

Nevertheless, the Church recognizes that mistakes do occur. It says if it be found that conditions existed that made true Christian marriage impossible, the bishop (sometimes with the advice of ecclesiastical court) may declare the fact and pronounce the marriage null and void. Then (of course, after requisite civil proceedings) the parties to it may be free, in the eyes of the Church, to contract a valid marriage.

The Church further provides that the bishop may review a marriage entered into contrary to the Church's canons, and gives him the authority, if he is satisfied that the best interests of the parties and of the Church require it, to restore the man and woman to good standing in the Church, which they have forfeited by their defiance of its laws. Justice, in short, may be tempered with mercy.

Exceptional cases cannot be decided by individuals or even by the parish priest. They are reserved to the bishop, who under the canons of the Church must exercise his right as the Father in God of all his children, and be the guardian of the Faith and authority of the Church. Most bishops take their responsibility seriously, and will not relax the discipline of the Church except for serious cause. The rule of the Church remains the injunction of its Lord: those whom God has joined together, no man may rightly put asunder. *Christian* marriage is for life—period. It is as simple as that—and it always has been—and always will be.

In modern Western society, the pattern of divorce and remarriage has increasingly become a socially acceptable way of life, but it cannot, and I say so emphatically, ever be a Christian way of life. Some thirty years ago, a certain king found that the Church still upheld the Christian standard, and lost his crown because of it. The Church does not have one standard for men in high public office and another for those in private life—as even a candidate for President may discover. The same high standard of family integrity is required of all who profess and call themselves Christians.

One of the great difficulties in some of our Church schools is teaching the children that God is like a loving father. If their own father and mother are not loving, how are they to form the right ideas about God? If they never see their parents at prayer, how are they to learn that prayer is important? If their parents are never in Church, how are they to know that Church is important? If their parents and their brothers and sisters are constantly arguing and bickering, how can they know anything about the loving and forgiving family of God? Any judge will tell you that most delinquent children come from broken families or from homes in which the parents are constantly quarreling—and that is as true of wealthy families as of poor ones.

The Christian family is intended to be a haven of changelessness in a changing society. It is, of course, subject to the common hazards of sickness, accident, and death, but it is nevertheless the environment into which children are born and should provide them with the love and security that they need and that God demands we give them. There is no sounder foundation for a natural, normal life than the Christian home. Christian homes do not come about without effort on the part of the parents, however. Love does not endure without cultivation and constant renewal; and our Lord never promised that Christian marriage would not be subject to all sorts of stresses and strains. On the contrary, illness, poverty, and the weakness common to mankind are foreshadowed in the marriage vow itself; but the relationship is "till death us do part."

In a former day, the family was rooted in the community, and the accidents of one family were in a measure shared by all. Today the average family may have to tear up its local roots every few years, and set them down in some new community, as best it can: rootlessness, constant change, is a phenomenon of our age, and the end of it is not in sight. It is one of the facts of life, and we have to learn to live with it.

In a society constantly on the move, the children are the ones who suffer most from lack of roots. Fortunately, with the universality of public school education, they may get a fairly good basic education in secular subjects, but even then there are exceptions. For example, children comprehend history and government by watching their parents participate in the local scene—"the consent of the governed." The child who is constantly on the move may end up with a knowledge of the geographical nature of his country, but with little understanding of his country's origin, of the growth and development of freedom, or of the source of its strength and its greatness. The old idea of patriotism, of responsibility for carrying on the ideals and the struggles of our forefathers for liberty under law, is fast being lost.

When some American prisoners of war in Korea were brainwashed by the Communists, our nation was shocked and astonished. How could our young people, wearing the uniform of their country, so easily confuse democracy and Communism? Communists had relatively little to wash out of the prisoners' brains before implanting the seeds of totalitarianism and subversion; the Americans had little knowledge of what had made America a great nation, or the cost of that greatness purchased by the blood of their forefathers. Everything had been handed to them on a silver platter—that is, until they were drafted into the armed service of a country of which they had little real knowledge and to which they felt only a mom's-apple-pie loyalty.

If patriotism has been a casualty of our roving, and rather shallow, way of life, Christianity has suffered even more. Ask the average young person to define Christianity, and his answer will be as vague as it is meaningless. At best he may think of it as an attribute of the "good life"—or even as a part of what he considers the "American way"—a luxury akin to television and motorcars and airplanes and jukeboxes. At worst, he may think of the Christian religion as a repressive force, something that prevents him from doing some of the things he would like to do, or at least from enjoying them fully. Many youngsters—and in this they are not unlike their elders—confuse true religion with a form of puritanism (and here I am thinking of smoking, drinking, and sexual mores). They may accede to certain current social standards or they may rebel; but never for a moment does it occur to them that Christianity is not defined by these guides to conduct.

Christianity is a way of life not only for those who have achieved a measure of sanctity but also, and more important, for sinners— for men and women and children of all sorts and conditions. Christianity is a society of imperfect human beings living together under conditions of ease or hardship, wealth or poverty, privilege or privation; it is fallen mankind trying to be raised a little higher, not by its bootstraps but by the grace of God; and the Christian family is the place where children learn the basic precepts of Christian life—or at least it should be so.

The family can look to the public or private school for the teaching of reading, writing, and arithmetic (fortunate is the child who begins to acquire those basic skills within the family), but it cannot look to the school, at least the public school, for guidance in religion—and that was true even before the Supreme Court ruled prayer and Bible reading out of the curriculum, where in fact it never had a large or effective place.

Neither can the family look exclusively to the church school for the teaching of religion. The Sunday school teacher finds it difficult or impossible to implant in half an hour a week the idea of God as a loving father if the child's own father has deserted his mother, or if his home life consists of a constant bickering among father, mother, and the children. How can the child be taught the importance of prayer, if there are no prayers at home—if his parents never pray, never say grace, nor teach him, long before he is ready for school, to kneel in prayer at his father's or mother's side?

The father is the priest of his own household, and the mother has a share in that priesthood. It is always proper for the father to ask God's blessing at meals, even though the parish priest or the bishop be a guest. He may ask such a visitor to say grace, but by doing so he extends a privilege, not a right. For purposes of instruction and because prayer is the right and privilege of every Christian, he may ask one of the children to do so; but if the father never exercises his right of priesthood in the home, the child is likely to gain the idea that prayer is something for children but not for grown men and women; and as he grows older he will put away prayer with other "childish" things.

Even more basic to the Christian family than spoken prayer is the inner prayer called Christian love. It is said that when St. John, the "beloved disciple" of Christ, became too old to go into the highways and preach, and perhaps had to be carried to someone's home for the celebration of the sacred Mysteries, his only sermon consisted of one sentence: "Children, love one another." Yet in that simple message he was summing up the essence of Christianity: God is love, and the expression of Christian love is the most faithful reflection of divinity.

In a truly Christian household, love is the cornerstone. The child must know from earliest infancy that his father and mother love each other, and that he is loved by them. His return of that love will be as natural as breathing. Christian love within the family is the basis of all future spiritual growth; it can become so strong that sickness and accident and even death cannot destroy it.

Love, like everything that is worth while, does not come without conscious effort. It is not to be confused with sentimentality, or lack of discipline, or mere absence of hostility. Love, especially Christian love, is a precious thing, and it must be cultivated in season and out if it is to endure and become an unbreakable bond. The child soon learns that his waywardness, his selfishness, his disobedience, may bring firm discipline and even punishment, but that it does not destroy the love that his father and mother have for him, and that they expect him to have for them and for his brothers and sisters.

In no case does love mean that the child is to be left undisciplined, or that he is always to be given his own way. It is part of the tragedy of American family life that it has often been allowed to become so child-centered that discipline collapses. A family in which the child is king is a problem for the parents and a menace in the community. Children want to know what they should do, even though they may sometimes reject it and rebel against it— even as you and I may do. The child wants to be told, and he can be happy only if he knows what is expected of him, and comes to learn that the expectation is reasonable, fair, and loving.

If, however, the parents are overly permissive, if they make idle threats that they have no intention of carrying out, or if they permit the child to play off one parent against the other, they will soon find themselves with a major disciplinary problem on their hands; and if they fail to mend their ways, they may find themselves with a family that is dominated by the children—a situation just as bad as that of a family in which the parents are arbitrary, cruel, and unjust.

I do not want to set myself up as an amateur Dr. Spock, and certainly I have no exceptional knowledge about the raising of children. In fact, the older I get, the less I know about it. But as a father and grandfather and as an observer of human relationships, this I do know: the family in which parents and children know their respective duties and responsibilities and in which the whole relationship is bound together with Christian love is a happy family. The devil and all his works cannot prevail against it.

Christian education, then, should begin in the home, and the family should be the center of Christian nurture throughout life. The child should be taught to pray as soon as he can talk; indeed talking with his heavenly Father should be as natural as talking with his natural parents and with other persons. Parents should never laugh at his childish prayers, nor think them irreverent, but teach him as early as possible the great pattern of prayer given us by our Lord himself. They should not wait until he goes to Sunday school for him to learn the habit of prayer.

Don't be concerned if his concept of God is a childish one, but help him to gain a more mature concept as he grows older. Never teach him anything that has to be unlearned. Keep the God-truth and the Santa Claus myth separate, so that when he learns that there is no Santa Claus, he won't jump to the conclusion that there is no God either.

Teach him some of the great Bible stories, and especially the story of the birth of Jesus—the shepherds and the wise men, the visit to the temple, the care of his blessed mother and of his foster-father St. Joseph. Teach him also about our Lord as the strong Son of God who brought life and healing and hope to the people with whom he came into contact. Don't let our Lord remain always a little child. I think the idea of itsy-bitsy altars and the sentimentality that often surrounds the cult of the baby Jesus can, if carried too far, inoculate the child against his understanding of our Lord as true God and true man.

Take the child with you to church, as soon as he is old enough to remain reasonably quiet. (An occasional wail or exclamation won't disturb the congregation, especially at an early celebration.)

If it is the parish custom, take him with you to the altar rail, to be blessed by the priest as he administers the Holy Communion. I know that some of the clergy dislike this custom, and that in some dioceses it is forbidden, but I think it is a good custom. It helps the child learn to feel at home in his Father's house, and to know that the Church cares about him as an individual.

The custom of having a family service, preferably the Holy Communion, at 9:00 or 9:30 has been encouraged in the Episcopal Church; and in many parishes it has become the one most widely attended. Often the church school is held at the same hour, and the older children may share in a part of the service and then go to their classes. It can be a great help to the parents, who are thereby relieved of extra driving on Sunday morning; but it has some drawbacks too. For one thing, it tends to break down the ancient and valuable self-discipline of receiving the Holy Communion fasting. For another, it confronts the parish concerned about music with a decision. Is the senior choir to participate at the later service which has few worshipers, while the junior choir sings at the larger service, the family service? There is nothing sacred about the hour of 11 o'clock. In the long run, the priest can generally determine what hours are best for his particular congregation, and schedule the services accordingly. In hot countries, the early service is sometimes at daybreak, with a later one at 8 or 9 o'clock, before the heat of the day. In most American communities, an early celebration of the Holy Communion is held at 7:30 or 8:00, a family service at 9:00 or 9:30, and the late service (fast becoming a shortened form of Morning Prayer and the Holy Eucharist) at 10:30 or 11:00. The important thing is for the services to be scheduled at convenient times for the congregation; the congregation should not be forced into the mold of a preconceived pattern of service.

It is unfortunate that Evening Prayer, or Evensong, has had to be abandoned in most parishes. It simply does not seem to fit the normal pattern of American life. In recent years, however, some parishes have found that an Evensong one Sunday a month is both possible and increasingly popular.

Here I would put in a plea for weekday celebrations of the Holy Communion, especially at an early hour. Many parish priests will say that they have tried daily celebrations, but that nobody comes. That may often be true at first, though it ought to be possible to find one person to promise to come each day, or an acolyte to serve. In parishes in which there is a regular daily service at, say, 7 o'clock, over a period of time people do begin to come, often for urgent personal reasons. It may be a birthday or a wedding anniversary, or the date of the death of a loved one. It may be that a businessman or a housewife, faced with a difficult problem that day feels the need of the special strength that comes from reception of the blessed Sacrament with special intention. There may be those in the parish who will undertake to be present one day a week, just to assure a congregation; if boys do not volunteer to serve at an early weekday service, the men in the parish can become a strong core of faithful acolytes. If no one comes, it is at least a good time for the priest to say his morning office and to intercede for the families of his parish. If more of our lay people would ask for weekday services, and volunteer to be present at least once or twice a month, most priests would be only too glad to provide them.

We have been speaking of the Christian family primarily in relation to the parish church and to religious practices within the home; but life is not lived primarily in the church building. Life is lived in the office and factory, the school and the supermarket, and in all the daily encounters of one individual with another. It is in those many activities, which make up so much of life, that Christianity exercises its influence. The Christian goes to church not as an end in itself but as a means to gain strength and inspiration for his secular life. True, we worship God in order to put first things first; but thereby we set the pattern by which our daily life will be governed. God is not interested only in what goes on in church. The world is his and he made it. He put us into it for a purpose, which is no less than to share in his creation. We glorify God in doing our daily work well; we are to serve him not only (or even primarily) with our words but with our deeds. The Benedictines have a phrase for it: *Labore est orare*—to work is to pray. The Catechism, now relegated to the back of the Prayer Book, says it even better: "To do my duty in that state of life unto which it shall please God to call me."

The layman is not called to be an amateur or part-time priest. He is called to be an expert and full-time Christian. He cannot be a Christian on Sundays and a pagan the rest of the week. His life and thought must have a consistent pattern, solidly rooted in the principles taught by our Lord, recorded in Holy Scriptures, and perpetuated in the Church.

Sometimes critics of Christianity point out that many men who have no connection with the Church actually lead better, more constructive lives than do many who profess and call themselves Christians. To our shame, that is often true; but it is not a far-reaching criticism. For one thing, those outside the Church (if they are really outside it, a theological question with which we shall not deal here) are drawing upon the accumulated spiritual capital of two thousand years of Christian tradition, and of many more centuries of God's dealing with mankind. For another, as we have said before, the Church is not a society of saints but a living organism, made up of sinners who nevertheless comprise the family of Christ.

We are members not only of one another but also, in St. Paul's vivid image, members of the Body of Christ. Certainly there are hypocrites among us, and there is a little hypocrisy in each of us. Certainly there are failures among us; one of the original twelve apostles betrayed Christ, only one stood by the cross. Certainly there are doubters among us; did not St. Thomas refuse to believe in the risen Christ until he could touch with his hands the wounds that he had seen inflicted on Christ's body? (In every age there have been Christians, even priests and bishops, who have doubted or denied or even betrayed our Lord.) Each one of us betrays him when we sin, however lightly; indeed by our sins we do even worse, we crucify him.

There have been times in the history of Christianity when the human manifestation of the Church militant was corrupt. There have been popes and cardinals who were notoriously evil. The Church constantly stands under the judgment of God, and needs continual reformation and renewal. Nevertheless, the promise of Christ stands, that the gates of hell shall not prevail against it. The holy Catholic Church, even when it stands in greatest need of reform, is his family and the certain manifestation of his earthly Body.

You and I, as baptized and confirmed laymen, are integral parts of that Body. Our vocation differs in kind from that of the bishops, priests, and deacons; but we, too, are set apart for his service. We are a part of the family of God. We share in his divine commission to go into all the world and make disciples of all nations.

The world into which we go may be the business world, or the academic world, or the world of science; it may be the world of everyday routine, of little things, of small choices; but every choice that we make is a choice for or against God, and the sum of the choices we make equals the personal character that each of us must build.

If charity begins at home, so does our share in the divine commission. I must accept my commission to be a disciple, a follower of our Lord, before I can extend that discipleship to others. I must do all in my power, with the help of God, to make my family a Christian one, before I can go into my world, however large or small it may be, and bring others into the household of faith.

Neither charity nor discipleship can remain at home, or it will sooner or later wither away. I must live as a Christian seven days a week, 365 days a year (and one more in leap years), for as many years as are given to me in this life—yes, and in the life to come, too, for the grave is not the end.

Fortunately, however, I do not have to do everything all at

once, or by myself. It is enough to live one day at a time, each day as if it were the only one, depending on the power of God, the protection of the angels, the prayers of the saints, and the support and forgiveness of my Christian brothers. I shall make mistakes, of course. I shall sin, and sin again, but God does not leave me helpless, and he is ever ready to forgive the sins of those who are penitent.

Almighty God, our heavenly Father, who settest the solitary in families; We commend to thy continual care the homes in which thy people dwell [and especially our home and family]. Put far from them, we beseech thee, every root of bitterness, the desire of vain-glory, and the pride of life. Fill them with faith, virtue, knowledge, temperance, patience, godliness. Knit together in constant affection those who, in holy wedlock, have been made one flesh; turn the heart of the fathers to the children, and the heart of the children to the fathers; and so enkindle fervent charity among us all, that we be evermore kindly affectioned with brotherly love; through Jesus Christ our Lord. *Amen.*

(Prayer Book, page 598)

Communism and
Anti-Communism

CHAPTER TWELVE

THERE is a general agreement that today Communism is the greatest threat to our way of life. We no longer have to look so far away as Soviet Russia or red China, or even to Berlin, to observe the growing menace in action. The Communists are in full swing only ninety miles off our Florida coast—in Castro's Cuba, a state which is avowedly Communistic, a state whose tyrannical government takes the lives of its citizens at will, a state where the lucky citizens become refugees reaching the haven of Miami. Many South American countries are riddled with Communism, and the reds are powerful right across the Rio Grande in Mexico. The external threat of Communism is no longer a far distant one; it is right on our own borders.

In the United States, too, the Communists, both foreign and domestic, pursue their constantly changing yet ever-basically-the-same line of subversion, espionage, and treason. Although the Communist Party is required to register as a foreign agency, its leaders are at large and constantly working underground against the best interests of our nation and our Christian faith. As usual, they work mostly through front organizations, wherever possible getting innocent but naive individuals to do their dirty work for them. Even the Church is not entirely free from insidious infiltration, although the irresponsible charges sometimes made that the Churches are riddled with Communists and fellow travelers do not bear the light of careful investigation.

It cannot be said too often that Communism and Christianity

are poles apart, and as different from one another as night and day. Communism is atheistic and man-centered; Christianity is religious and God-centered. Communism represses the individual in the supposed interest of the state or of mass man; Christianity raises the individual and makes him the child of God. Communism would destroy free institutions, despite its perverted use of the word *democracy;* Christianity is the very bulwark of our free society. Communism follows the devious pathways of darkness; Christianity follows the way of Jesus Christ, the Light of the world. The motivating force of Communism is hate; the motivating force of Christianity is love.

The contrast of motives and methods must be clear to all thinking Christians, and there can be no doubt where the convinced Christian must stand. The real difficulty, however, comes when we consider what to do about the struggle between the powers of darkness and the powers of light. It is easy to get into a state of panic and attempt to fight the powers of darkness with the weapons of evil.

The Christian cannot be a true follower of the Prince of Light if he pursues the way of darkness. He cannot be a faithful soldier and servant of the God of love if he relies upon hatred to accomplish his aims.

There is not one great commandment but two: to love God and to love our fellow man. Our Lord went even further; he taught us also to love our enemies. That does not mean that we should be undiscriminating in our love, or that we should fail to recognize our enemies as such; but it does mean that our warfare must be against the powers and principalities of evil, rather than against the men and women who often are their victims rather than their advocates.

General Shoup, the commandant of the United States Marine Corps, made it quite plain when he said recently: "Our basic teaching for young Marines is love of our own country, our own way of life. Of course we illustrate the forces that seem to be opposed to our way of life—and nobody should have any trouble seeing the contrast. If you are devoid of ideals, ignorant of the Christian way of life, then you are simply stumbling in a morass, and to be told the evils of the other side cannot have any lasting impression on you. It was not hate that sustained the U.S. prisoners in Korea, but faith and confidence."

Another distinguished American, General Alfred M. Gruenther, emphasized the importance of individual responsibility in the struggle: "From the days of our youth we have learned that in a democracy such as ours, government derives its powers from the individual. Under totalitarianism the government is supreme, and the individual may be given certain rights only as the government chooses. Of course, there can be no doubt in our minds as to the desirability of the democratic method. But that system will not operate by itself. It could fail, as other free societies throughout history have failed, if the sense of individual responsibility is lost."

The Episcopal Church is clearly and unmistakably on record in opposition to Communism, both foreign and domestic, as a denial of the very basis of Christianity and a subverting of the Christian way of life. Here are the exact words of the official reaffirmation of this position adopted unanimously by the House of Bishops and the House of Deputies in the 1961 General Convention:

Whereas, the Christian faith teaches us to strive and suffer for unity, freedom, and peace among men; and that God's will is related to all of life; and

Whereas, Marxist Communism is a false, atheistic religion, hostile to man's fullest freedom, destroying the self-determination of peoples, intent on world domination and, therefore, threatening the peace of the world; and

Whereas, The pressure of the international Communist menace can lead to hysteria, divisiveness, suspicion, and a tragic disunity of people in the hour of crisis; and

Whereas, The Protestant Episcopal Church in the United States of America through its leaders and official teachings has always taken a

clear stand in opposition to all tyrannies that crush the human spirit;
therefore, be it

Resolved, That the 60th General Convention of the Protestant Episcopal Church in the United States of America reaffirms its opposition to
atheistic Marxist Communism; and be it further Resolved, That, aware
of those problems in human life on which Communism feeds, this General Convention renews the call of the 1948 Lambeth Conference, which
includes this statement: "It is the special duty of the Church to oppose
the challenge of the Marxian theory of Communism by sound teaching
and the example of a better way, and the Church at all times and in all
places should be a fearless witness against political, social, and economic
injustice."

A stronger statement of the essential incompatability of Christianity and Communism could hardly be made. But, you may say,
it is easy to make a high-sounding statement of general principles:
what is the Church actually doing to make those principles effective in the Church and in society?

That, my friends, brings the problem right down to your door-
step, for you and I and all the baptized persons registered on the
books of our parishes and missions are the Church.

General Convention is not the Church. The bishops and other
clergy are not the Church. The building in which you worship on
Sunday is not the Church. The Church includes all of them
but it is much greater than any of them, or the sum total of them.
The Church, as defined in the Offices of Instruction, is "the Body
of which Jesus Christ is the head and all baptized people are the
members." *The Church is the Body of Christ.* It is also, in a mys-
terious sense, the *body of the faithful,* the men, women, and children
who make up its human membership. So when you say, "What is
the Church doing about this or that problem," you are actually
asking, "What am *I* doing about the problem?"

I have pointed out that the Episcopal Church is clearly on
record against Communism and have cited the resolution of General
Convention to that effect. The Church is also on record as to the

wrong way to fight Communism. As to this let me quote a second resolution adopted by the General Convention of 1961:

Resolved, That this General Convention reaffirms the declaration of the House of Bishops of 1947, that "the people of our Church be on their guard lest an hysterical fear of Communism should lead us to fight that danger with weapons destructive of the treasures we seek to guard. The surest way to fight Communism is to work unceasingly at home and abroad for a society in which justice and the dignity of free men are in truth guaranteed to men of every race and condition; and be it further Resolved, That the people of our Church be cautioned to examine carefully charges of disloyalty and subversion brought by extremist groups, and the oversimplified appraisal of our situation which they promote, lest fear and suspicion destroy honest public debate and silence the expression of Christian faith in human affairs."

Charges have been made from the time of Senator Joseph McCarthy to the present, that the churches are riddled with Communists in high places and that their softness toward Communism is an effective point of entry for Communist propaganda. Not only have such charges never been proved, but the fact is that Communists have found the churches almost impossible to infiltrate by their customary methods.

Undoubtedly the Communists have tried to infiltrate the ranks of the clergy, but they have found that it is much easier said than done. Louis Cassels, a well-informed Washington correspondent, wrote in *The Episcopalian* (July, 1961):

As a practical matter, it is enormously difficult for a Communist to pose convincingly as a dedicated Christian even for the space of one conversation, let alone through the long years of seminary study and pulpit service which are required of any man who becomes an influential leader in U.S. Church life.

Later in the same article Mr. Cassels quoted FBI Chief Inspector William C. Sullivan in a speech delivered in many parts of the nation, warning Americans not to be taken in by charges that their churches are infested with hidden Reds.

These allegations have served to create the impression among many Americans that the Protestant denominations in particular have been subjected to alarming infiltration and influence, but this is a patent falsehood. The truth of the matter is that the Communist party has not achieved any substantial success in exerting domination, contol, or influence over America's clergymen or religious institutions on a national scale. America's religious institutions are one of our most formidable bulwarks in the crusade against Communism. There can be no question as to the loyalty of the overwhelming majority of the American clergy to the nation, and the fact that they have been among the most consistent and vigorous opponents of Communism.

Similar findings have been published by the Roman Catholics and the Presbyterians as a result of their study of the alleged infiltration of their churches by Communists.

Somewhat more successful has been the Communist campaign to dupe well-meaning Christian clergymen into lending their names to Communist-front projects. And that is something against which all Christians should be on their guard. Unfortunately, however, some members of the clergy, including some in the Episcopal Church, seem to be unable to resist the temptation to sign their names to a petition or appeal or statement which may seem innocent on its face but which plays into the hands of the Communists. It is easy, for example, in our horror of the threat of nuclear warfare to be duped into signing a petition calling upon the President and the United States Government to abolish its stockpile of nuclear weapons and to begin the process of disarmament unilaterally. Why such petitions are never addressed to the Soviet dictator by the same individuals is a matter beyond my comprehension, except that it is obvious that such a petition would never get past the Kremlin mail desk.

The Churchmen, particularly in the Episcopal Church, who lend their names to such documents are very few; most of these are so well known as rather fuzzy-minded pseudoliberals that their signatures are worthless. No doubt they are well intentioned and presumably will have their reward; but loyal Churchpeople should be on their guard not to be overinfluenced by them. Give them an *F* for effort but do not make the mistake of assuming that they are the real leaders of the Church.

How then can the Church and individual Churchmen effectively combat the menace of Communism?

I am not speaking now of Christians in high places in government, although thank God there are many distinguished leaders in the administration, in the Senate and House of Representatives (of both parties), and on the Supreme Court bench who are guided by Christian principles. Certainly, we should uphold the hands of such men, from the President on down; and certainly when we come to exercise the privilege of the ballot we should try to vote for men who, whether professing Church membership or not, will be guided by the basic principles of the Old and New Testaments, the foundation of our free society.

I am thinking primarily of what you and I as ordinary Christians can do in our own communities, and particularly through our own parishes, to make the witness of the Church effective in such important areas of national and civic concern.

The important thing to remember, it seems to me, is that Communism not only stirs up social unrest but that it thrives upon social injustice and turns the weakness of our social institutions into social, economic, and racial strife. If we are to prevent that —and we can—the Church should be foremost in its effort to remedy whatever may be unjust or wrong in our own society, and not simply to leave it to other agencies, official or unofficial, to do so.

One of the major problems in New York, for example, is housing—much is ramshackle, insanitary, totally inadequate, and overpriced. Some of the leaders among our clergy, notably the Rev. James A. Gusweller and the Rev. C. Kilmer Myers, fully supported by their congregations and by the Bishop and Diocesan Convention, have turned the spotlight on the festering evil of our city and in many instances have succeeded in forcing a reluctant city administration to take remedial steps. This is true Christian social action, requiring courage and Christian perception with the wisdom to keep it on a Christian plane and to prevent deterioration into mere political maneuvering. The result is that thousands of depressed and oppressed New Yorkers know that they have an understanding friend in the nearest Episcopal church, and they are not entirely dependent on the local ward boss. Nor are they so inclined to turn to Communist leadership in the hope of righting their wrongs.

Let me summarize from the National Council of Churches *Handbook on Communism*[1] three important things that the Church does to carry out its social responsibilities:

1. The Church holds up the ideal standard of Christ and the Christian conscience as the best measure of all social systems.

2. The Church educates its members on the problems and needs of society as seen from the vantage point of Christian conscience. It encourages individual and group action by responsible Christian citizens along social, economic, and political lines.

3. The Church provides a center of love and strength for its members as they seek to advance the cause of Christ in their own community and other places. Each of these areas of action enfolds a great variety of possibilities.

Some of you may rise up and say, "The National Council of Churches does not speak for us"; and others may go further and say, "The National Council of Churches itself is heavily shot through with Communism or at least with a liberalism that makes it an easy dupe of the Communists."

To that I would reply: how sure are you of your facts? Are not those three basic principles in accord with the resolutions of our own General Convention? "By their fruits ye shall know them."

When I was elected president of the House of Deputies in 1961, the first day I was deluged with telegrams of congratulation from all over the country. The next day I had more stacks of telegrams, but these were on a different subject. The gist of them was: "Get us out of the National Council of Churches." Most of them did not say why, and many of them were signed by such vague designations as "ten members of the Episcopal Church." A good many of them were suspiciously similar in their text, indicating that they might emanate from some pressure group.

Within the General Convention itself there was some agitation for withdrawal from the National Council of Churches, although happily on a more moderate and reasonable basis. We gave full consideration to the matter through a series of open hearings and a free debate on the floor of the House of Deputies. The result was a unanimous resolution, the nub of which was the following:

Resolved, That the Joint Commission on Ecumenical Relations be instructed to make a study of the Structure, Program and Finances of the National Council of Churches of Christ in the United States of America with special reference to the following matters:

1. The content, adoption procedure, and publication of pronouncements, statements, educational literature, reading lists, and the like;

2. The method of appointment or election of our representatives;

3. Increasing the quorum of the General Board; and to report results of such study, with its recommendations, to the next General Convention.

That study of the National Council of Churches has been made under the competent leadership of the Very Rev. Gray M. Blandy, Dean of the Episcopal Seminary of the Southwest. Some of the members of the committee were initially favorable to the National Council of Churches, others were opposed to it; but they came out with a unanimous report, not whitewashing the National Council of Churches but clearing it of the charge of subversion and indeed praising it for its effective opposition to Communism. The report is well worth reading by those who will do so with an open mind.

Certainly it is true that the National Council of Churches does not speak for the Episcopal Church, except insofar as the official representatives of the Episcopal Church participate in its actions and try to carry out the mandates of our General Convention. It is also true, however, that, generally speaking, the so-called pronouncements of the National Council of Churches are parallel to the resolutions of our own General Convention, and certainly there are many areas in which the Christian churches working together can be far more effective than any one of them alone.

A good example is found in the whole organization of Church World Service and also the work among refugees from Communist countries. We may take particular pride—if we can do so in a Christian way—in the manner in which our Church is helping to resettle and relocate refugees from Cuba who are constantly arriving in Florida. Our own Diocese of South Florida, aided by our National Council, is doing great work in the field despite inadequate resources of personnel and finance. Other dioceses from as far away as California and Ohio have sponsored "flights in freedom" in an effort to resettle some one hundred thousand Cuban refugees in other parts of the country under the auspices of our Church. There is genuine Christianity in action.

No, our churches are not infiltrated with Communism, though there is always the danger that Communists may try to pervert them for their own use. Many of our parishes, however, are victims of even greater evils; they are permeated with dullness and self-satisfaction, well content to operate as religious enclaves, having little or no contact with the problems of their communities, or of the nation and the world; they are in short infiltrated by the world and the devil—the creeping sickness that is constantly racking the Body of Christ.

The parish is the local representative of the whole Church in its community. Nothing that concerns the community should be foreign to the interests of the Church. The best witness of the parish against Communism is to *be the Church* in its community —to be concerned with problems of housing, social injustice, racial discrimination, and the other insidious evils that infiltrate all our communities, large and small. They are the festering sores that nourish domestic Communism. The Church cannot be indifferent to them if it is true to its divine nature and calling.

Almighty God, who hast created man in thine own image; Grant us grace fearlessly to contend against evil, and to make no peace with oppression; and, that we may reverently use our freedom, help us to employ it in the maintenance of justice among men and nations, to the glory of thy holy Name; through Jesus Christ, our Lord. *Amen.*

(Prayer Book, page 44)

War and Peace

CHAPTER THIRTEEN

I APPROACH this chapter with trepidation, for the problem with which it deals is the greatest one that faces this world, and it becomes more perplexing and threatening every day.

America finds itself faced with a dilemma by its nuclear capabilities, and by the equal capabilities of our potential enemy; so we are trapped in a situation from which there seems no immediate escape.

Today we have the power to destroy Russia—and all the world. Russia has the ability to destroy America—and all the world. Tomorrow Communist China may have the ability to destroy both Russia and America—and all the world.

In a series of articles in the Scripps-Howard newspapers in June, 1963, Henry J. Taylor surveyed the nuclear stockpile situation in the United States and came up with some appalling facts. There are, he said, "five enormous nuclear fountains feeding our overkill stockpile." They are at Oak Ridge, Tennessee; Hanford, Washington; Paducah, Kentucky; Portsmouth, Ohio; Savannah River, South Carolina. He adds: "Taxpayers have invested five and a half billion dollars on these alone."

Each of the plants has been producing nuclear weapons at a cost of two billion dollars a year. The stockpile in 1963, Taylor says, was already enough to kill everyone in the world living in a city of 100,000 or more, *125 times over.*

What are we going to do with all that destructive material? Why do we continue to add to it? How could we destroy it if we wanted to do so?

The American Christian is faced with a real dilemma. As an American he wants to be sure that his nation is adequately protected from all enemies, foreign or domestic. He is ready to fight, if necessary for the preservation of his country, and the positive values for which it stands.

I do not know why I put this in the third person. I fully subscribe to that attitude. In World War II, through some of the bloodiest battles in the Pacific, I wore the uniform of my country. If war came again, and I were not too old, I would dig my uniform out of the closet, darn the moth holes in it, and wear it again, for whatever duty my country might require of me.

But war is no longer the way it was then. We are told that a new war might be over in forty-eight hours and that few would survive it, regardless of who won it. Moreover, those who did survive would find the land so devastated that the conditions under which they would have to live would bear little resemblance to the civilization we know.

As a Christian, I am prepared to agree with the statement frequently made by our House of Bishops (between wars) that war is "incompatible with Christianity." Yet, as a Christian, I know also that death is not the greatest evil. For my own part I should rather be dead than red—to use a popular phrase in some circles—but I am not sure that I have the right to make the same choice for my children, grandchildren, and great-grandchildren.

In the spring of 1962 I attended a conference called to deal with the Christian attitude toward war and to draft a statement for the House of Bishops. We were a mixed group—some pacifists, some militant nonpacifists, and some who were simply perplexed. The result of our deliberations, which ultimately turned up in a statement issued by the House of Bishops at Columbia, South Carolina, on November 1, 1962, reflects the uncertainty. The bishops endorsed our findings, but the findings were wordy, involved, and inconclusive.

Following the promulgation of the statement by the House of

Bishops, the Division of Christian Citizenship of the National Council organized meetings all over the country to discuss it. I attended none of them nor have I read any of their findings, but I suspect they were as inconclusive as the document drafted by us and issued by the House of Bishops.

Yet there are some good things in the report. The best part of it is the statement of the theological basis of our concern, stemming from belief in God who is sovereign over all men. "For a Christian there is no loyalty which transcends his loyalty to the will of God. No earthly state is omnipotent. Before God all men and all nations stand under judgment. . . . Our Lord died for Russians, East Indians and Chinese, as well as for Americans." [1]

I believe all that, but it doesn't help me much in making up my mind about the great questions of war and peace in our modern society. I'm not sure that it would help the President of the United States or the Chairman of the Joint Chiefs of Staff, who are also Christians. In any case, what can I, an ordinary citizen, do about it? There seem to be about six major approaches to this problem —and I am not sure that I could subscribe to any of them.

1. There is the pacifist approach. It is the easiest to understand. The pacifist will not bear arms in any war in any circumstance. It is an understandable position but one that I believe to be unrealistic and in the present day and age nationally suicidal. I cannot go along with it.

2. There is the nuclear-pacifist approach. Those who follow that pattern would say that they would fight in ordinary wars but not in a nuclear war. They would have the United States disarm unilaterally. That is also suicidal and I cannot go along with it.

3. There is the ostrich approach—those who would bury their heads in the sand and not face the problem at all, but leave the whole matter to chance or to whatever administration may be in power. I suspect that most Americans belong to this category, although I doubt if many would admit it. Certainly it solves no problems.

4. There are the advocates of preventive war—the people who urge, for example, that we should invade Cuba and get rid of Castro. It is an appealing project, but I strongly suspect that if we attempted it the fat would be in the fire and the ultimate result would be the nuclear war that we all want to avoid. Moreover, I cannot see such a policy as compatible with Christianity. I cannot go along with that position.

5. There are the advocates of limited war, the use of only small tactical nuclear weapons. The difficulty with such an approach is that there is no way to guarantee that the war will remain limited. To be sure, we fought such a war in Korea and we are fighting another in Viet-Nam; but the results are inconclusive and unsatisfactory. Moreover, there is always the danger that the limited war will become a general war, and then again our fat would be in the nuclear fire.

6. There are the advocates of massive retaliation. This was the policy formulated by the late John Foster Dulles, and although there is more talk now of controlled reaction to provocation, I suspect the Dulles policy is still the basis of our military posture. The trouble with it is that we could lose most of our centers of population and industry in the enemy's first strike, and our retaliatory strike would simply compound the problem, with the probable result that both nations would be destroyed.

Pope John XXIII, in his notable encyclical *Pacem in Terris* issued just two months before his death, stated:

The production of arms is allegedly justified on the grounds that in present-day conditions peace cannot be preserved without an equal balance of armaments. And so, if one country increases its armaments, others feel the need to do the same. And if one country is equipped with nuclear weapons, other countries must produce their own, equally destructive. . . . Justice, right reason and humanity, therefore, urgently demand that the arms race should cease; that the stockpiles which exist in various countries should be reduced equally and simultaneously by the parties concerned; that nuclear weapons should be banned; and that a general agreement should eventually be reached about progressive disarmament and an effective method of control.[2]

With that aim, few men of good will would disagree. Perhaps the first step in that direction has been taken by the agreement between Russia, Britain, the United States, and other countries to suspend nuclear tests in the atmosphere. There are, however, others in the "nuclear club" to whom the treaty will not apply, notably France, and perhaps in the near future, Communist China. Moreover, as we noted at the beginning of this chapter, the United States, and presumably Soviet Russia also, already have more than enough nuclear weapons to destroy humanity, and more are being added every day. Is there no way to break this inexorable procession toward disaster? What can the individual do about it? Pope John deals with this problem in another part of the encyclical:

. . . In traditionally Christian nations, secular institutions, although demonstrating a high degree of scientific and technical perfection and efficiency in achieving their respective ends, not infrequently are but slightly affected by Christian motivation or inspiration. . . . It is necessary, therefore, that their interior unity be re-established, and that in their temporal activity faith should be present as a beacon to give light, and charity as a force to give life. . . . It is indispensable, therefore, that in the training of youth, education should be complete and without interruption; that is to say, religious values should be cultivated in the minds of the young and their moral conscience refined in a manner to keep pace with the continuous and ever more abundant assimilation of scientific and technical knowledge. And it is indispensable, too, that they be instructed regarding the proper way to carry out their actual tasks.

In other words, Christians should be trained to live like Christians, and express Christianity in their lives. True, but what of the many who do not do so, and of the millions who do not even profess to be Christians? What of the nations that are devoted to godless Communism, and who are determined to root out the human values for which Christianity stands?

What are the implications of this sound doctrine for a loyal and patriotic American who honestly wants to act as a Christian but finds the problem too big and too insoluble for the individual?

I don't pretend to know the answer. What bothers me most, however, is that so few people seem interested in asking the question and in trying to find an answer. We shall not begin to find a solution until we honestly face up to the problem.[3]

There are, however, two things that I firmly believe. One is that, as Americans, we must not choose the way of war, which is the way of destruction. We must defend our liberties and our way of life (even though it is by no means a perfect one), but we can do so successfully only by peaceful means.

The other thing I know as a Christian: we cannot give in to despair. Curiously enough, *Life* magazine, December 14, 1962, making the same point, gave the reasons for it more clearly than the statement of the House of Bishops, the papal encyclical, or any other religious pronouncement that I have read:

One type of man may be apprehensive but never desperate; the believing Christian. Why? First, because despair is the one unforgivable sin; to indulge it is to deny that Christ died to save us all. There is another reason. Christians, most of them, have a rather special view of human history. They believe that human history has an Author and a plot, with a meaningful, not a meaningless, end.

Quoting our Lord's words, "Lo, I am with you always, even unto the end of the world," *Life* continues:

The Christian view of history is providential. God has intervened, he is history's Lord; and all the apparent causes of events on earth, from human nature and intelligence to the laws of chance, are in reality vehicles of divine will. God not only created this world, he is still creating it, with human help. Said the late scientist-Jesuit Teilhard de Chardin: "In action I cleave to the creative power of God . . . I become not only its instrument but its living promulgation." The Christian can no more foresee the future than other humans, nor is he necessarily a better judge of the consequences of his own acts. But at least he can use his gifts, his time, and his reason with the confidence that no act is wasted for in all human endeavor some portion of the divine purpose is being fulfilled.

In other words, if we claim to be Christians we must *act* as Christians both nationally and personally, and leave the outcome in the hands of God. The Rev. Gardiner M. Day, in a sermon preached at Christ Church, Cambridge, Massachusetts, on May 26, 1963, spelled out the Christian responsibility and the Christian hope as follows:

. . . Our Christian insight should enable us to keep from being overwhelmed by a sense of helplessness and hopelessness and becoming cynical. . . . As long as man has been on the planet he has faced forces far greater than himself. Had we lived in the first few thousand years in the life of mankind we would have been very much aware of the titanic natural forces such as floods caused by the sudden overflowing of a river. Now man faces enormous man-created forces, but I believe that we can still have faith that just as man has learned to control flood waters by constructing dams and reservoirs, so he will learn to control these man-made forces that have fallen into his hands. We can be sustained in all our work and thought for peace by our conviction that God has not abdicated; that God reigns and that God still wants all men "to have life and to have it abundantly" (John 10:10), and specifically this means the building of a world community in which all men have access to every resource of human welfare, that St. John's vision of a new heaven and a new earth may become a reality (Revelation 21).

That may not seem a very satisfactory solution; indeed, in human terms it is not a solution. It is an expression of Christian hope and faith in God.

No man living today would dare project his thoughts one hundred years hence and predict what the world will be like at that time—if indeed there be a world of people at all. Curiously, though, I believe that there will be a world one hundred years from now and that it will be a better world than the one of today. I think my great-grandchildren will have life, and I pray that they may have it more abundantly than we who live under the shadow of nuclear death.

If I were asked the reason for my hope and belief, I could only reply that I trust God and that I believe that history is the working out of God's purpose. Our Lord gave some indication of that purpose when he said: "I come that you may have life and that you may have it more abundantly."

In the days of Theodore Roosevelt, when it seemed clear that our nation had a manifold destiny to perform, there was a slogan: "Fear God and keep your powder dry." I suggest as a slogan for Christian Americans today: "Trust God and keep your missiles under control."

Almighty God, who has given us this good land for our heritage; We humbly beseech thee that we may always prove ourselves a people mindful of thy favour and glad to do thy will. Bless our land with honourable industry, sound learning, and pure manners. Save us from violence, discord, and confusion; from pride and arrogancy, and from every evil way. Defend our liberties, and fashion into one united people the multitudes brought hither out of many kindreds and tongues. Endue with the spirit of wisdom those to whom in thy Name we entrust the authority of government, that there may be justice and peace at home, and that, through obedience to thy law, we may show forth thy praise among the nations of the earth. In the time of prosperity, fill our hearts with thankfulness, and in the day of trouble, suffer not our trust in thee to fail; all which we ask through Jesus Christ our Lord. *Amen.*

(Prayer Book, page 36)

The Church and Segregation

CHAPTER FOURTEEN

PERHAPS the greatest blot on the record of the Church in the twentieth century has been its failure to take real leadership toward the abolition of racial segregation. Today we are in the midst of a full-fledged cultural revolution in which the colored citizens of the United States are demanding their full rights as citizens and Christians—rights long denied them by both state and Church. At long last white Americans are beginning to realize the truth of Abraham Lincoln's dictum that a nation cannot long endure half slave and half free. True, the slaves were freed one hundred years ago, but they were freed only to become second-class citizens. Now, a century later, they are demanding their rights as first-class citizens. Their demand must be heard and accepted promptly if our nation is to continue as a truly United States.

My concern in this book is not primarily with the civil rights of members of minority races, although these are closely linked with their rights and responsibilities as individuals and as Christians. My major concern is with the failure of the Church—of all Christian bodies—to take leadership in the field, and in effect to trail behind the federal and many state governments, thus negating the principle that the Christian way of life arises from the teachings of our Lord and the clear record of Holy Scriptures.

St. Paul wrote to the Galatians: "For ye are all the children of God by faith in Christ Jesus. For as many of you as have been baptized into Christ have put on Christ. There is neither Jew nor Greek, there is neither bond nor free, there is neither male nor female: for ye are all one in Christ Jesus. And if ye be Christ's

then are ye Abraham's seed, and heirs according to the promise."
(Gal. 3:26-29)

St. Paul was not merely expressing a theory; he was writing
to a mixed group of Christians, some of them Jewish, some Gentile,
some free, some slave. Christianity in the first three centuries spread
most rapidly among the slaves of the Roman Empire, largely because only in the Church were the slaves able to find the inner
freedom and dignity that made it possible for them to realize the
full measure of their manhood. Thus in the Christian gospel itself
lay the seeds of freedom and of the equality of all men.

Throughout the ages the gospel of freedom has been preached,
but only too often it has been neglected in practice. The idea of
a segregated church with separate parishes and institutions for
men of different race and color would have been incomprehensible
to St. Paul, and we may be quite certain that it is abhorrent today
to the living Christ, who is the Lord of the Church.

To be sure, the Church in the twentieth century has not been
without its ringing pronouncements on the equality of all men.
One could cite resolutions of the Lambeth Conference, the Anglican Congress, the General Convention of the Episcopal Church,
the Assemblies of the National, and World, Council of Churches,
and many another high-level ecclesiastical body making noble statements of policy; but the actual practice of the Church has lagged
far behind.

The racial situation in the Church's own parishes and institutions is, in fact, a challenge to its integrity. In spite of much recent
soul-searching and no little improvement in practice, a Negro priest
can still charge that in this country "the Church is a segregated
and segregating body." He adds: "Christians ought not to be
surprised that judgment begins with the household of God." [1]

Surely the time has come—indeed is long overdue—when the
Church should eliminate all vestiges of racial segregation in all of
its parishes and institutions. That is a minimum, not a maximum.
Beyond that the Church should be positively at work to serve mem-

bers of minority races, to welcome them into its fellowship, and to make them an integral part of its structure at all levels—parochial, diocesan, and national.

A part of the failure of the Episcopal Church has been its reluctance to make more positive efforts to preach the gospel to all men, regardless of racial or national origin. We have been too much the Church of the white Anglo-Saxon American, the Church of the upper and middle classes, the Church of the well-born and well-to-do.

Our Church came to America with the first settlers at Jamestown in 1607. It had a great opportunity to become the Church of the American people. It lost that opportunity when it allied itself with the ruling classes in colonial days, when it neglected the immigrants of the eighteenth and nineteenth centuries, when it ignored the stranger in our midst and was content to be the Church of the "best people." We have therefore become a minority Church; one which only within the past few decades has welcomed into its fold people of other than English ancestry and the Caucasian race.

The Episcopal Church has, however, resisted the tendency to split into racial bodies. There is no "African P.E. Church" or "Colored Episcopal Church"; there are only Episcopalians of African descent and of the colored races. At least our segregation has been within the Church rather than by forcing Negro Episcopalians to form a church of their own.

Perhaps the reason that we have avoided a denominational segregation is not entirely to our credit. I have often visited dioceses in the deep South where I have been told that there is no racial problem, only to find the reason—there are so few Negro Episcopalians. Why is this? Simply because the Churchmen of that area have been content to be a privileged minority and have made little or no attempt to bring into the Church either Negroes or those whom they consider "poor white trash."

Never was that sad state more dramatically illustrated than it was in the murder of the Mississippi NAACP representative Medgar Evers, allegedly by a man who had been considered a representative Episcopalian of good family and fine connections. How had such a man been able to attend Church regularly and still gain such a warped concept of the Christian religion?

The Presiding Bishop, Arthur Lichtenberger, made clear the difference between the Church's official position and its failure to act upon the principles enunciated by official bodies in a strong statement made in the spring of 1963, later endorsed by the House of Bishops. He wrote:

Our Church's position on racial inclusiveness within its own body and its responsibility for racial justice in society has been made clear on many occasions by the General Convention. But there is urgent need to demonstrate by specific actions what God has laid on us. Such actions must move beyond expressions of corporate penitence for our failures to an unmistakable identification of the Church, at all levels of its life, with those who are victims of oppression. . . . It is not enough for the Church to exhort men to be good. Men, women and children are today risking their livelihood and their lives in protesting for their rights. We must support and strengthen their protest in every way possible, rather than give support to the forces of resistance by our silence. It should be a cause of rejoicing to the Christian community that Negro Americans and oppressed peoples everywhere are displaying a heightened sense of human dignity in their refusal to accept second class citizenship any longer.

The right to vote, to eat a hamburger where you want to, to have a decent job, to live in a house fit for habitation: these are not rights to be litigated or negotiated. It is our shame that demonstrations must be carried out to win them. These constitutional rights *belong* to the Negro as to the white, because we are all men and we are all citizens. The white man needs to recognize this if he is to preserve his own humanity. It is a mark of the inversion of values in our society that those who today struggle to make the American experiment a reality through their protest are accused of disturbing the peace—and that more often than not the Church remains silent on this, our greatest domestic moral crisis.

Bishop Lichtenberger called us to involve ourselves in such matters as housing, employment, public accommodations, and schools; to give money as an expression of our unity and as a sign of our support for the end of racial injustice; and to take action to end segregation within the Church's own ranks. He wrote:

Discrimination within the Body of the Church itself is an intolerable scandal. Every congregation has a continuing need to examine its own life and to renew those efforts necessary to insure its inclusiveness fully. Diocesan and church-related agencies, schools, and other institutions also have a considerable distance to go in bringing their practices up to the standard of the clear position of the Church on race.

Thus the Presiding Bishop has called upon the Church in unmistakable terms to desegregate our own parishes and institutions. It is an important step and a long overdue one, but it is still only a first step toward setting our own house in order.

The next step—and one that should be taken simultaneously —is to go beyond the passive acceptance of Negro communicants and to make a real effort to bring Negroes into the Church. There is a great opportunity for our Negro priests, many of whom are fine, well-educated individuals but who have not shown notable qualities of leadership in extending the Church among members of their own race. But it is the responsibility of white Christians, too.

We should like to see every parish—north or south, located in an area in which Negroes live—make a real evangelistic effort to bring as many as possible of them into the parish fellowship and life of the Church.

Once their own position is clarified and they know that they are truly welcome in the Church, Negro priests and laymen must take more responsibility for the extension of the Church among their own people. They alone can perform the task in the transition period through which the Church is passing in this time of social revolution. We need many more of them, and we need greater recognition of them, not as shepherds of a minority but as priests of the Church of God, called to minister to the people of God, of whatever race or color.

There is also a great burden placed upon Negro citizens generally to take upon themselves the responsibilities as well as the privileges of first-class citizenship. Laws properly enforced can give them the rights that have been lacking to them in the past, but with every right goes a corresponding duty. The responsibility of good citizenship rests squarely upon the shoulders of those to whom legal and social rights are extended.

Martin Luther King, a truly great Christian and citizen, has based his campaign of passive resistance on the truly Christian principle that rights also involve duties and responsibility. In a letter written from a Birmingham jail and published in *The Christian Century* (June 12, 1963), he answered those who object to sit-in demonstrations and similar nonviolent protests by the statement that "we have not made a single gain in civil rights without determined legal and nonviolent pressure." In a poignant paragraph on what segregation has meant to Negroes, he wrote:

We have waited for more than 340 years for our constitutional and God-given rights. The nations of Asia and Africa are moving with jet-like speed toward gaining political independence, but we still creep at horse-and-buggy pace toward gaining a cup of coffee at a lunch counter. Perhaps it is easy for those who have never felt the stinging darts of segregation to say, "Wait." But when you have seen vicious mobs lynch your mothers and fathers at will and drown your sisters and brothers at whim; when you have seen hate-filled policemen curse, kick, and even kill your black brothers and sisters with impunity; when you see the vast majority of your 20 million Negro brothers smothering in an air-tight cage of poverty in the midst of an affluent society; when you suddenly find your tongue twisted as you seek to explain to your six-year-old daughter why she can't go to the public amusement park that has just been advertised on television, and see tears welling up when she is told that Funtown is closed to colored children, and see ominous clouds of inferiority beginning to form in her little mental sky, and see her beginning to distort her personality by unconsciously developing a bitterness toward white people; when you have to concoct an answer for a five-year-old son asking, "Daddy, why do white people treat colored people so mean?"; when you take a cross-country drive and find it necessary to sleep night after night in the uncomfortable corners of your automobile because no motel will accept you; when you are humiliated day in and day out by nagging signs reading WHITE and COLORED; when your first name becomes "nigger," your middle name becomes "boy" (however old you are) and your last name becomes "John," and your wife and mother are never given the respected title "Mrs."; when you are harried by day and haunted by night by the fact that you are a Negro, never quite knowing what to expect next, and are plagued with inner fears and outer resentments; when you are forever fighting a degenerating sense of "nobodiness"—then you will understand why we find it difficult to wait. There comes a time when the cup of endurance runs over, and men are no longer willing to be plunged into an abyss of injustice where they experience the bleakness of corroding despair. I hope, sirs, you can understand our legitimate and unavoidable impatience.

Writing of the role of the Church in this cultural revolution, Dr. King contrasted the vigor of the early Church with the ineffectual part that he sees it playing today:

There was a time when the Church was very powerful—in the time when the early Christians rejoiced at being deemed worthy to suffer for what they believed. In those days the Church was not merely a thermometer that recorded the mores of society. Whenever the early Christians entered a town the power structure immediately sought to convict them for being "disturbers of the peace" and "outside agitators." But the Christians pressed on, in the conviction that they were "a colony of heaven," called to obey God rather than man. Small in number, they were big in commitment. By their effort and example they brought an end to such ancient evils as infanticide and gladiatorial contests.

Things are different now. So often the contemporary Church is a weak, ineffectual voice with an uncertain sound. So often it is an archdefender of the status quo. Far from being disturbed by the presence of the Church, the power structure of the average community is consoled by the Church's silent—and often even vocal—sanction of things as they are.

But the judgment of God is upon the Church as never before. If today's Church does not recapture the sacrificial spirit of the early

Church, it will lose its authenticity, forfeit the loyalty of millions, and be dismissed as an irrelevant social club with no meaning for the 20th century.

I confess that I felt much the same when, upon invitation of President John F. Kennedy, I attended a White House conference of religious leaders called to discuss the subject of civil rights. I could not help but feel that it should have been the Church calling the nation to repentance, in the stern words of Isaiah or in the loving precepts of our Lord, rather than the state calling upon the Church for help in promoting social justice!

A prophetic work in the field of race relations in the United States was *An American Dilemma,* by Gunnar Myrdal, a study financed by the Carnegie Corporation, originally published in 1942. In an anniversary edition twenty years later, one of the author's associates, Arnold Rose, observed:

There could be no doubt that the races were moving rapidly toward equality and desegregation by 1962. In retrospect, the change of the preceding twenty years appeared as one of the most rapid in the history of human relations. Much of the old segregation and discrimination remained in the Deep South, and housing segregation with its concomitants was still found throughout the country, but the all-encompassing caste system had been broken everywhere. Prejudice as an attitude was still common, but racism as a comprehensive ideology was maintained by only a few. The change had been so rapid, and caste and racism so debilitated, that I venture to predict the end of all formal segregation and discrimination within a decade, and the decline of informal segregation and discrimination so that it would be a mere shadow in two decades. . . . The dynamic social forces creating inequality will, I predict, be practically eliminated in three decades[2]— [i.e. by 1992].

Mr. Rose concedes that most sociologists would find these predictions too optimistic, but adds: "Most sociologists found the predictions contained in *An American Dilemma* of twenty years ago optimistic, and most of those predictions have since come true."

If the prediction of Mr. Rose is to come true, it will only be as the result of intensive efforts by white and colored citizens alike. Both will have to learn to exercise more responsible citizenship, better understanding, and greater charity than ever before. Not only must whites and Negroes learn to understand one another better, but each must learn to be more charitable and understanding of his own people. James Meredith, whose courage had opened the doors of the University of Mississippi to Negro students, deplored mob action in attempting to attain Negro rights; Negroes did not help their cause when they denounced him. Black Muslims and other groups that preach hatred and advocate Negro superiority are as dangerous as the Ku Klux Klan and other groups that preach hatred and advocate white superiority.

We must recognize also that the problem is not a sectional one, but a national concern. In the same week that 200,000 citizens, white and colored, staged a great peaceful demonstration for civil rights in Washington, a white mob in Pennsylvania hurled insults, rocks, and firebrands at a Negro family trying to move into a house in a suburban development. Discrimination in employment is as rampant in New York and Chicago as it is in the deep South; and it is not easy for a colored family to find adequate housing in Boston or San Francisco.

Again, there is the need for greater responsibility on both sides. Whites must be willing to work side by side with Negroes, and to admit them gladly to the highest positions for which they may be qualified. Negroes must prove themselves good workers if they are to have more important jobs; they must prove themselves good neighbors if they are to achieve better housing. Standards of family life are notoriously low among Americans of colored ancestry; this, too, is a problem to which they must address themselves.

In all of these matters, the Church can be of great help. In a phrase frequently misinterpreted, our Lord said to his followers: "Ye are the salt of the earth." He did not mean that they were the best people; he meant that their task was to impregnate and flavor the society in which they were set, as he clearly implied in the rest

particularly concerned about the matters of bias and discrimination directed against his black children.

The time for resolutions of General Convention is past. We have on our books all the resolutions that we need. What is required now is the courage to put the Christian religion of love into effect in every parish of our Church, North and South, East and West, at home and overseas. Let's stop talking about race and get on with our job of bringing all men, women, and children to God.

O Eternal God, through whose mighty power our fathers won their liberties of old; Grant, we beseech thee, that we and all people of this land may have grace to maintain these liberties in righteousness and peace; through Jesus Christ our Lord. *Amen.*

(Prayer Book, page 263)

The Church Looks to the Future

CHAPTER FIFTEEN

ANGLICANS TO VANISH, THEY HEAR —so read a headline in a New York paper reporting one session of the Anglican Congress held in Toronto in August, 1963. The prediction, made by a bishop who likes to make dramatic statements, is premature. It may be true, as the bishop explained, that "the vocation of the Anglican Communion is to disappear"—eventually, in the growth of Anglicanism into a wider Catholic unity—but meanwhile the Episcopal Church and the other Anglican churches are very much alive and have much to do together, as the Congress itself made clear.

Specifically, as the Anglican Congress pointed out in its major declaration of policy: "Our professed nature as a world-wide fellowship of national and regional Churches has suddenly become a reality. . . . The keynotes of our time are equality, interdependence, mutual responsibility."

"Three central truths at the heart of our faith," the statement continued, command us in this:

The Church's mission is response to the living God who in his love creates, reveals, judges, redeems, fulfills. It is he who moves through history to teach and to save, who calls us to receive his love, to learn, to obey, and to follow.

Our unity in Christ, expressed in our full communion, is the most profound bond among us, in all our political and racial and cultural diversity.

The time has fully come when this unity and interdependence must find a completely new level of expression and corporate obedience. Our need is therefore not simply to be expressed in greater generosity by those who have money and men to spare. Our need is rather to understand how God has led us, through the sometimes painful history of our time, to see the gifts of freedom and communion in their great terms, and to live up to them. If we are not responsible stewards of what Christ has given us, we will lose even what we have.

The Archbishop of Canterbury summed up the situation more succinctly: "The Church that lives to itself will die by itself."

The Anglican Congress proposed, therefore, that there be greater cooperation between Anglican churches, with frequent consultation and common planning for missionary work throughout the world. Along with this would go "a comprehensive study of needs and resources . . . to give us up-to-date, tested data on actual work now going on, resources in manpower (clerical and lay), training facilities, financial resources and their distribution, and the unevangelized areas which still confront the Church." This study will require that each Church join in "immediate commitment for increased support in money and manpower, through existing new channels, in cooperation with the other Churches of our communion," and that "every Church seek to test and evaluate every activity in its life by the test of mission and service to others, in our following after Christ." The statement concludes:

We are aware that such a program as we propose, if it is seen in its true size and accepted, will mean the death of much that is familiar about our churches now. It will mean radical change in our priorities— even leading us to share with others at least as much as we spend on ourselves. . . . In substance, what we are really asking is the rebirth of the Anglican Communion, which means the death of many old things but—infinitely more—the birth of entirely new relationships. We regard this as the essential task before the Churches of the Anglican Communion now.

The program set forth by the Anglican Congress includes the following five points:

1. A meeting of the primates and metropolitans (heads of national churches and provinces) every two years.

2. The appointment of regional officers, in Africa, the British

Isles, India, Pakistan and the Middle East, the South Pacific, and South East Asia, working under the leadership of the executive officer (Bishop Bayne and his successor).

3. Frequent meetings of the Advisory Council on Missionary Strategy to collect and distribute information on resources and needs.

4. A substantial common fund—$15,000,000 in the next five years—to meet existing and pressing needs.

5. A new way of thinking and acting, based on the equality and independence of each national Church—the young and the older together—and their unity and interdependence in mission.

What does all this mean to the Episcopal Church in the United States—to its General Convention and National Council, its dioceses and parishes, and the rank and file of its membership? It may mean much or little, depending upon our response; but certainly it means that there is a great deal that we are called upon to do before our Church vanishes, disappears, or becomes absorbed into some future but not yet foreseeable "Great Church." And if such a wider unity does come about, the task of going into all the world to preach, to teach, and to reconcile sinners to God will still remain.

The Anglican Communion is not a Church; it is a federation of churches holding the same faith and united in one communion and fellowship. The Anglican Congress is not a legislative body. It cannot pass laws or set policy for the eighteen self-governing churches that make up the Anglican Communion. Anglicanism has no pope, no vatican, no central governing body. The Archbishop of Canterbury has a primacy of honor, but he has no jurisdiction outside his own province, and no authority outside the Church of England. How, then, are we to achieve the "radical change in our priorities" to which the Anglican Congress calls us?

So far as the American Episcopal Church is concerned, if the recommendations are to be translated into action, it will be the General Convention that will have to set the pace and determine the new priorities. It will require us to take a new look at our missionary program, at home and abroad; at our policies in social relations, in religious education, in urban and rural work, in theological training, and in every aspect of our national and world-wide work. It will require formulation of new policies, and the translation of them into terms of program and budget. It will compel us to re-think the basic question of the mission and function of the Episcopal Church, and its relationship to Anglicanism, to other Christian bodies (both Catholic and Protestant), to our nation, and to the world.

Our dioceses and our parishes will also have to do some hard thinking about their tasks and their relationship to the whole Church. As the Toronto statement said, by way of illustration, "a new organ in Lagos or New York . . . might mean that twelve fewer priests are trained in Asia or Latin America." The Archbishop of Canterbury pinpointed it further when he observed that perhaps our parishes will have to learn to give away at least as much as they spend on themselves.

The first place in which the Episcopal Church will have to begin its task of "agonizing reappraisal" is at the top. The National Council, through forty-five years of bureaucratic growth, has developed an immense establishment of officers, directors, and staff now housed in a magnificent ten-story Episcopal Church Center a block or two from the United Nations Plaza in New York. Its work is divided into Overseas and Home departments, departments of Christian Education, Christian Social Relations, Promotion, and Finance; general divisions of Laymen's Work, of Women's Work, and of Research and Field Study. There is a general secretary for Evangelism, an ecumenical officer, and an executive officer for Strategic Planning. The machinery is modern, and the wheels turn busily. It has been said that four whole provinces in Africa could be completely rehabilitated by the dozens of bishops and priests, the scores of executives, and the hundreds of workers within the center, together with the thousands of dollars required for its operation.

Certainly we need adequate organization and good business

administration for a Church of three and a half million members. It sometimes seems, however, that all this machinery is too concerned with keeping its own wheels turning, and that some of its key people are not in tune with the currents of change that are sweeping through the world and the Church. These changes threaten to make many of our old-fashioned methods irrelevant.

From time to time an attempt is made to bring a new look into the Church's national policies and planning, apart from the day-by-day administration of its far-flung operations, but with only moderate success. Such an attempt was the Committee on Overseas Policy and Strategy, headed by Bishop Gray of Connecticut, which made a constructive report to the National Council several years ago. More recently, a Strategic Advisory Committee has tried to take a new look at certain policies and plans of the National Council; but in the three years of its existence it has been largely frustrated.

Now the Anglican Congress has given a clear mandate to the Episcopal Church, and to other churches of the Anglican Communion, to raise our sights, look farther ahead, and do some real strategic planning; to pool our resources and apply them where they are most needed and where they have the best chance of success.

Overseas, three areas particularly cry out for attention. In Africa, the rise of dozens of new nations, the renaissance of Islam, the social and technological revolutions, and the threat of Communism make a rethinking of the Christian mission on that continent imperative. The African provinces of the Church desperately need the help and support of Anglicanism in Britain and America, but it must be clearly divorced from the kind of ecclesiastical colonialism that has prevailed in the past. We must learn to help them to help themselves; to train their clergy, educate their young people, and improve their health and general welfare. But the time has passed when we can do so on the basis of sending out missionaries to run their churches and institutions. They want to develop their own leadership, even if they make many mistakes in the process—just as we have made.

In Latin America the needs are somewhat different, but no less pressing. We are barely beginning to face the question: what (if any) is the role of Anglicanism in a Latin culture? The American Church has been at work for many years, in Puerto Rico, Haiti, Cuba, Mexico, Brazil, and elsewhere. More recently we have undertaken work in Peru, Colombia, and Ecuador. The English Church has generally been content with chaplaincies to English-speaking people in South America. Surely, if we have any mission in these countries, it should be the witness of a Catholic Church free from the domination of Rome, which can be a rallying point for their own cultural and spiritual traditions. Is this a worthy objective? If so, how do we set about to accomplish it?

In southeast Asia, again the needs are different. We are beginning to face them in the Philippines, through our full communion and united work with the Philippine Independent Church, which may lead to a great resurgence of faith and the development of a truly indigenous national Catholic Church in that country. We are learning also to work there with the United Church of Christ in the educational field, and to cooperate with the Roman Catholic Church, rather than to fight it, in making the Philippines more truly Christian. We need something of the same kind of program in Malaysia and among the Chinese of the dispersion all along the rim of Asia.

It is imperative that we rethink and reorient our whole overseas mission program, now, before doors open to us are slammed in our faces. The Macedonian call to "come over and help us" is as loud today as it was in New Testament times, and our Lord's command to preach the gospel to all nations is as valid today as it ever was. But the methods that worked in the nineteenth century and the first half of the twentieth century are no longer the methods that we can or should use today. We desperately need a new look at the Church and the world, and at the way in which our own Church—not alone, but in company with other Churches both within and without the Anglican fellowship—can best respond to that call and that command today.

If we need a new look at the mission of the Church overseas, it is even more true that we need a new look at the mission of the Church right here in the United States of America. Here, too, the currents of change run deep and strong.

Is religion banned from the public schools? Then we must look to strengthening it in the home and in the parish. Is urban growth and industrialization forcing "our people" from the cities to the suburbs? Then we must find new ways of filling the void in the cities, for the denizens of the factories and the offices in megalopolis are also God's people and, therefore, ours. Does apartment living and a constantly shifting population make old parochial methods impossible? Then we must devise new methods to fit new situations.

Our very concept of the nature of the ministry and of theological education needs restudy and prayerful rethinking. In recent years an increasing number of priests have been drawn from the business, industrial, scientific, and educational world. Some exercise a dual ministry—as priest and scientist, or priest and teacher. Should we encourage more dual vocations of this nature, more worker-priests, more industrial priests? If so, how are we to train them, and how should our parish and diocesan life be modified to utilize their special skills?

What about our young people? How can we cope with the falling away of adolescents after their confirmation? How can we challenge the best of them to enter the priesthood? What about vocations to religious orders? What about the parents, often active Church people themselves, who discourage their sons and daughters from vocations within the Church?

What has the Church to say, and what can it do, about the breakdown of family life, which is so prevalent today? Adultery, divorce, remarriage—this is the vicious cycle that is corrupting the heart of our society, alike among the rich, the middle-income, and the poor.

Where does the Church really stand in the perplexing question of race relations? Are we going to be content to drag our heels and leave the leadership to the government and to pressure organizations? When are we going to set our own house in order?

It is easy to raise these questions, and they could be multiplied indefinitely. Finding the answers is not so easy. These are the problems with which the Church must live and with which it must cope.

In a world of sin, of disillusion, of frustration and despair, the Church must still proclaim the message of our Lord: "I am come that ye may have life, and that ye may have it more abundantly."

Thank God, there are thousands of priests, thousands of ministers of all the Christian churches, and hundreds of thousands of lay people who are aware of these problems and who are doing their best to cope with them. Too often, however, they are discouraged at the very magnitude of the problems, and they often tend to withdraw from them.

Other churches are also undergoing the currents of change, including the Roman Catholic Church, hitherto considered as the very bastion of ultraconservatism. We were raised on the axiom that "Rome never changes." It is not true today. A good many radical changes were proposed at the Second Vatican Council, most of them apparently supported by an overwhelming majority of the assembled bishops.

It is surprising how many of these changes have a familiar ring to Episcopalians. One needs only a superficial acquaintance with the history of our own Church and the mother Church of England to see remarkable similarities. Are the Roman Catholics about to translate the Mass and other services into the vernacular? The Anglican Church did it four hundred years ago. Are they seeking to restore the chalice to the laity? This was one of the basic principles of the English Reformation. Are they trying to find a real place for the diaconate as a major order in its own right? So are we, and with the growing number of perpetual deacons and of lay readers we are approaching a solution to the problem of clergy shortage.

Are they trying to decentralize the administration of the Church? Here the Anglican pendulum is swinging the other way; we are trying to centralize or at least coordinate our world-wide strategic planning. Are the Roman Catholics seeking a more significant role for their laity? We have it at every level, from the parish to the General Convention and the Anglican Congress. The Church of Rome is even planning to invite women to participate in the Ecumenical Council. There they are ahead of us; we have not yet admitted women to our General Convention, but I hope we may soon do so.

Sometimes it seems that the Roman Catholics are becoming more Anglican than the Episcopalians. If so, we are all for it. But if we are not to be left behind, surely it is high time for Episcopalians to become more Catholic—to use more fully the treasures new and old that we have in our own Church. It is not enough for us to sit back complacently and point with pride to the liberties won for us by our fathers in the distant past. It is for us Churchmen of the second half of the twentieth century to make our own contribution to the modernization of the Church and its relevancy to the circumstances of our times.

We cannot leave the problem to the General Convention or the National Council or to our own bishops and priests. The task is one for all of us, including those of us whose vocation is that of the laity. For we laymen do have a vocation in the Church. Our calling is to *be* the Church, the people of God. We are, or should be, the cutting edge of the Church, the means by which it comes to grip with the problems of the world. Our place of operation is not the sanctuary, or even the nave of the Church. We go there, of course, for inspiration, for instruction, and for the strength that comes from prayer, from preaching and teaching, and from the strength of the sacramental life.

But the place in which we are called to live the Christian life, and to do our part in the bringing-in of the kingdom of God, is the marketplace, the office and the factory, the school and the home. We cannot, we dare not, try to be Christians on Sundays and pagans on weekdays. Our Lord warned us two thousand years ago: "No servant can serve two masters; for either he will hate the one and love the other, or he will be devoted to the one and despise the other. You cannot serve God and mammon." (Luke 16:13 RSV)

It is significant that Christ was not talking to the disciples when he said this, but to the Pharisees, the sharp businessmen of his day. And St. Luke, who recorded the conversation, observed that "the Pharisees, who were lovers of money, heard all this, and they scoffed at him." There are still plenty of money-lovers, both outside and inside the Church, who do the same today.

In most parishes, there is a small core of concerned people, surrounded by a large fringe of the indifferent. These latter are the fair-weather Churchmen. They want the parish church there so it will be handy for weddings, for christenings, for burials—though often they leave the last rites in the commercial hands of the "mortician" and the "funeral chapel." They send their children to Sunday school, and they attend church when it is convenient.

Fair-weather Christianity is not enough. It breaks down at the crucial times of life—at times of family troubles, of sickness, and of death. The fair-weather Christian may seem attractive, urbane, and civilized on the exterior; but under the shell of his complacency there is a great void. As someone has said: "He may be deep on the outside, but way down deep he's shallow."

Am I by any chance describing you? Am I describing myself? Honesty compels me to answer Yes to the second question, for there is some element of "fair-weather Christianity" in all of us. The Bible has a short, ugly word for it: *sin*. In a world in which other short, earthy words have a new vogue of popularity, this one is still unpopular—probably because it is so true and so much a part of each one of us.

I may seem to have gone far afield from my subject, "The

Church Looks to the Future." I have done so, however, by a series of logical steps; progression from the great general problems of the Church's organization and mission throughout the world to the small specific problem of you and me. It really boils down to that simple but disconcerting prayer: "Lord, revive thy Church, beginning with me." [1] That's where it all has to begin, isn't it?

The call to the Church to look to the future, to plan effectively, to increase its resources and to apply them wisely, is a call not only to the General Convention, the National Council, the diocese and the parish, but also a call to you and me. For, humanly speaking, you and I *are* the Church.

"The Church that lives to itself will die by itself," said the Archbishop of Canterbury. We can paraphrase it: "The Christian who lives to himself will die by himself." The Anglican Congress, in its final message, said: "God has moved us by His Holy Spirit to think very hard about our vocation as Christians. *Selfish ways must go.*"

The revival of the Church, the spread of Christ's kingdom at home and abroad, the discovery of new ways of ministry to the world's needs—all of this must begin with the average Christian, the sinner sealed with the sign of the cross in Baptism and nourished with the bread of life in Holy Communion. It's not just somebody else's job; it's yours and mine.

"Lord, revive thy Church, beginning with me."

The Church's Secret Weapon

CHAPTER SIXTEEN

WHEN I was mustered out of the Marine Corps, at the close of World War II, I went to live in a new community. One of the first things I did was to transfer myself and my family to the little mission church there and enter our children in the Sunday school. The next spring our youngest was enrolled in the Confirmation class, perhaps six or eight weeks before the bishop was to visit the church to minister that apostolic sacrament.

After one or two classes I questioned my son as to what he was learning in Confirmation class. "Not very much, dad," he replied candidly; and on questioning him further I found that it was in fact the case.

I went to see the priest to ask him why he was not giving the class a little more substantial training, and he gave me this strange reply: "I don't feel called upon to indoctrinate these young people." I am afraid I hit the ceiling. I remembered the long, arduous drills and instructions that I had received in my basic training in the Marine Corps, the nights when I would fall into bed bone tired only to be awakened at dawn for another day of the same strenuous training, which was quite frankly described as "indoctrination." I remembered further the frequently repeated observation of my drill sergeant: "The secret weapon of the Marine Corps is the well-trained Marine."

Surely, the same is true of the Church. Our secret weapon is the converted, well-trained, enthusiastic layman. Without this secret weapon the Church can be nothing but a religious club for the elect, but with it the parish becomes a powerful unit in the Church militant, ready to do battle in season and out with its ancient enemies: the world, the flesh, and the devil.

There is no province in the universal Church, Catholic or non-Catholic, in which the clergy and the laity so completely share the responsibility at every level of administration, as they do in the Episcopal Church. The parish cannot function without complete trust and cooperation between the rector and the vestry. The bishop cannot carry on the work of his diocese without the cooperation of the other clergy and laity in the Diocesan Convention; he cannot even ordain a man without the consent of his Standing Committee, half of whom are laymen. At the national level, our General Convention is made up of the House of Bishops and the House of Deputies, clerical and lay; neither house can enact legislation without the concurrence of the other. The Presiding Bishop carries on the top administration of the Church through the National Council, at least half of which consists of laymen and women.

There is no place for clericalism in the Episcopal Church. At the same time there is no place for a lay pope. Clergy and laity must work together at every stage if the work is to go forward. It is to the credit of the Church that this is so generally understood and assumed that a breakdown between the clergy and the laity is a rare event; but when it does happen the work of the Church in that community gradually grinds to a halt. Indeed, the parish in which such a breakdown occurs becomes a byword and a scandal among the people of the community.

If this is true of the Church's administration, why is it not equally true in carrying out the divine commission to go into all the world, to teach all nations, baptizing them and bringing them into the divine community? That was the great commandment of our Lord, given to his disciples with his promise to be with them always, even unto the end of the world. Obviously, therefore, it was not only for the chosen few but for all who would come after them throughout the ages. It is a commandment that applies to all Christians, not simply to the bishops or the ordained clergy, or for those who are professional missionaries.

In the great ages of the Church, the divine commission has always been so interpreted. It was probably laymen in the Roman Army and traders from the Mediterranean who first brought Christianity to Britain. It was Christian communities, and not simply the clergy, who built up the new world settlements at Jamestown and Plymouth. The Body of Christ has many members, and it is only when all of them function together that it is a whole and healthy organism. That is as true today in America as it was in the primitive Church when it spread out from Jerusalem to the west and east and eventually to all parts of the world.

We live today in a much more complicated world than that of the primitive Church or of any age that has gone before us. No longer, at least here in America, do we live in small communities where people know one another intimately and where the priest is "the parson" (person) of the village.

Our parishes reflect the diversity and complexity of our civilization. In the average parish, urban or suburban, the worshipers who come together on Sunday go their separate ways during the week, and there is little to bind them together as a community. Many of them live at a distance from the church in various parts of a large city, and do not even see each other between Sundays. Fortunate is the priest who can keep up with the various interests of his scattered parish and bring some measure of unity into their diversity.

It is easy to deplore our present complexity and diversity, but the situation is not entirely a deplorable one. Certainly, it opens up new horizons for the Church and gives point to new ways of ministering and new ways of reaching people *where they are* with the message of Christ.

A bishop in Ceylon was asked what the effect on the work of the Church would be if the schools were nationalized and Christian teachers were dispersed among public and non-Christian educational institutions. He replied that it could be the greatest stimulus to Christianity in that country if the Christian teachers would take with them their Christianity and radiate it to their non-Christian students, even though they were forbidden to teach Christianity itself.

That is a clear recognition of the value of the layman as the secret weapon of the Church. Properly understood, the layman spreads his faith not so much by *talking* Christianity as by *living* Christianity. If this is true in a non-Christian country like Ceylon, how much more true should it be in a country such as our own built on Christian principles now largely ignored?

Canon Carmichael, of St. Louis, was quoted recently as saying: "The ministry of the Christian layman is always performed, if at all, in the world where he works, where he lives, where he spends his ever-increasing recreational hours." He added: "In most instances the professional ministry of the Church has little more than a passing acquaintance with the peculiar issues and concerns that occupy the thought and attention of the members of a particular profession, trade, or discipline."

Here, it seems to me, is the clue to Christian ministry in a complex and secularized society. Except in a few instances, it is impossible for the priest to go himself into the factories, the offices, the schools, the labor unions, in which his people work and spend the major portion of their lives. Yet those are the very fields of combat between the Church and the world; those are the places in which victory is to be won in the name of Christ the king, or in which his banners are to go down to shameful defeat.

The answer is to be found in the use of the Church's secret weapon—its converted laymen, women, and children. On them falls the burden of the divine commission today, as indeed it has in the past and will until the end of the world.

If, however, the secret weapon is to be really effective, we have to find a way of breaking out of the shell of parochialism and of shedding the cloak of Sunday eleven o'clock respectability. We can no longer expect the masses of the people to come to the Church; we must take the Church to the people where they are.

We must somehow get away from the conventional attitude that the *essence* of Christianity is to go to church. In a very real sense we do not go to church; we *are* the Church. As we have noted before, the very word *laity* comes from the Greek word *laos,* which means "people"—specifically, the people of God.

The parish church is not the place in which the Christian life is lived. It is rather the powerhouse from which the layman obtains the grace, the strength, and the knowledge that enable him to live the Christian life in the world and to bring the Christian impact to bear upon its life.

We must get over the idea that the layman is the ultimate consumer of Christianity; he is rather its salesman and area representative. The breadth and the height and the depth of his Christianity is measured not by his pious attitude or his self-esteem but by the influence he has on those with whom he lives and moves and has his being.

I do not mean that we laymen should be expected to be self-generating powerhouses, able somehow to go it alone without guidance or direction. The ministry of the layman is not the same as the ministry of the priest: indeed, it is the layman himself who is first to object if the line between the two is blurred. As a simple example of this, I have only to point to two or three occasions when the laymen in General Convention turned down the proposal for lay administration of the chalice, though the bishops and many of the clergy voted in favor of it. The layman does not want to be an amateur priest, nor is this his proper function in the Body of Christ.

The layman rightly looks to the parish priest as his captain in the Christian warfare. He looks to him as his teacher in the Christian doctrines. He looks to him as his example in the Christian life. He looks to him as the one who ministers to him the sacred host and the consecrated chalice from which he derives his strength and his power both to live the Christian life and to radiate it to others.

When the priest stands at God's altar celebrating the divine Mysteries, he stands before the congregation as the representative of our Lord himself. It matters not whether his ceremonial is simple or elaborate, but whether it be reverent, dignified, and authoritative.

I welcome the trend to the Family Eucharist and to the effectiveness of the Liturgical Movement in bringing the Holy Eucharist closer to the people; but there is also a danger that must be guarded against. Perhaps I gave some hint of that when I purposely described the celebration of the Holy Communion in Eastern Orthodox terminology, "the Divine Mysteries." We lose much if in our endeavor to bring the Holy Table closer to God's people we rob it of that element of mystery which has been described as the numinous —the sense of reverent awe in the presence of the Most Holy.

I recall the great emphasis laid upon the necessity of mystery by the saintly priest who prepared me for Confirmation, and his constant reiteration of the phrase, "The church is an altar with a roof over it." I can still hear the voices of the children echoing the phrase after him. I don't think any one of them will ever forget that the altar is the center and focus of the Church's worship.

I have lived to join in the worship of God at many a great cathedral church throughout the world, at many a parish church large and small, and in many celebrations of Holy Communion under improvised conditions. During the war my altar was often the hood of a jeep or the tailgate of a military truck, or a table set up in the wardroom of a Navy ship. Once the altar was an abandoned Japanese supply case in a newly captured cave on Iwo Jima. (An hour after the service a Marine tried to pry the case open with his bayonet to see what was inside. It was booby-trapped, and in the resulting explosion he lost his hand.) In all of these services under the most diverse conditions one fact remained constant—our Lord was there under the sacramental forms of bread and wine, just as he had promised, to feed his children and give them strength for the tasks that lay before them.

For the Holy Eucharist, as Bishop Bayne points out in his book

Enter with Joy, "is not really a service, not really an act of worship at all, but rather an act of God which we mortals are only allowed to seek and to share." Yet in sharing it, we are indeed joining in the greatest act of worship, because we are sharing, in our human way, the mighty act of God in the redemption of the world through our Lord Jesus Christ. Here surely is the supreme service of the Church, the very point at which this world stands on the threshold of eternity.

If the altar is the center and heart of the Church, the pulpit is also of great importance, for there the word of God is preached, and there the priest has the solemn duty and privilege of teaching the Christian faith. It is far more important for a preacher to teach the faith and to apply it to the needs of his congregation than it is for him to be a great orator.

I would plead for more teaching sermons, in which the truths of our holy religion are set forth clearly and without compromise, without fear or favor or watering down in the hope of making them easier or more palatable, yet done at the same time with love and understanding.

If the priest has doubts about the Virgin Birth or some other aspect of the Church's faith, the pulpit is not the place to air them. Let him wrestle with his difficulties in private prayer and study, and take them to his bishop or to a priest of deep faith and wide experience for counsel and guidance.

I am well aware, as is every layman, that there are different ways of looking at the doctrines of the Church and that, to quote one distinguished bishop, "the old faith must be presented in new packages." Let us be sure, however, that we are not confusing the product with the package, or projecting our doubts on those who have difficulties enough themselves and who look to the clergy for solid teaching and not for fancy packages.

A layman's study committee in the Diocese of Maryland showed some understanding of the nature and purpose of the Church, and the weakness of much of our contemporary preaching and teaching, in a report now published by the Forward Movement under the title, *Laymen Look at the Laity*.

We believe that the Church is divinely instituted, guided, and drawn by God to manifest his saving purpose to the world. It is a fellowship in which the Good News is preached, its meaning apprehended and realized in the life of its members. Its essential purpose is to worship God and to announce and live the new creation in Christ. We believe the Christian life is free and joyful, and at the same time demanding, and challenging.

And yet, on many Christians the Church today makes little demand; it does not discipline, disturb or challenge them. Being a Christian is too easy. The Church seldom reminds that while Jesus was forgiving, winsome, merciful, and gentle, he was also disturbing, stirring, frank, startlingly direct, and accusatory. We don't like to be reminded of judgment, preferring to think it has been entirely supplanted by love and forgiveness, which some mistakenly think require no commitment, no service, no suffering. All too often the Church speaks in a tone of well meant advice rather than of eternal truth.

The Maryland laymen are right; the pulpit is the place for teaching the eternal truth, not for giving vague advice to men who are all too familiar with the problems of the business or professional world, but who rarely see them in the clear light of the revelation of our Lord and the experience and teaching of the Church.

If this is true of preaching to adults, it is even more true of teaching in the Church school and in Confirmation classes. I have little patience with the theory that the Christian faith should somehow be distilled out of the limited experiences of children through the method of discussions and buzz groups, or whatever the current terminology may be.

Whatever else Christianity is, it is a religion that was revealed to man by the prophets and evangelists, and by our Lord Jesus Christ himself. True, it was built upon the experiences of the people; but to their own experience was added the revelation of almighty God, without which his people would never have found him.

It is all very well to meet the child where he is and to build upon his experiences, but for God's sake—I say it reverently—don't stop there. That is the beginning and not the end of Christian education.

Finally and in summary, I hope you will permit me, as a layman who knows more members of the clergy in the Episcopal Church than most laymen, to pay a tribute to our clergy as a whole.

It is still true that members of the Episcopal Church's clergy are men of learning and, for the most part, men of wisdom; more important, they are men of great sincerity and personal devotion.

We laymen do honor and admire our priests, whether we call them "Father" or "Mister," or just plain Joe. We love them, we look up to them, and we are confident that they will give us guidance and leadership in full measure of their priesthood.

I think many laymen are far more ready than clergymen realize to be trained and sent out into the world as representatives of Christ and his Church. Charles Parlin, distinguished Methodist layman and one of the presidents of the World Council of Churches, observed recently that the ecumenical movement and the Second Vatican Council have awakened a new interest in religion on the part of laymen of all churches. That interest has somehow broken the lines of division to an extent that at last laymen can talk with one another about the deeper things of our common religion. "Those things," says Mr. Parlin, "have opened up vast new opportunities for a layman to speak to a layman about the Christian faith and the affairs of the churches. The topic of religion is no longer taboo. He can speak where he works and where he has his social contacts. In the teamwork of clergy and laity, here is the new and great opportunity for the lay people of the Christian Church." If this is true among Christians, it is also true between convinced and nominal Christian laymen, between believing Christians and those who have fallen away altogether.

Laymen are indeed the secret weapon of the Church—but only

laymen who are informed, convinced, and converted. We must be laymen who know and love our Church, and who try to lead a truly Christian life.

A Christian life must be a disciplined life. We do not come by it easily, thoughtlessly, or without prayer and careful planning. The best way is to have a rule of life—not an idealistic and impractical one, but one worked out in accordance with one's own particular circumstances, and revised from time to time to reflect one's own spiritual progress or lack of it.

The Anglican Church of Canada, in its recent revision of the Book of Common Prayer, made the idea of a rule of life a definite part of the commitment of its members:

Every Christian man or woman should from time to time frame for himself a Rule of Life in accordance with the precepts of the Gospel and the faith and order of the Church; wherein he may consider the following:

The regularity of his attendance at public worship and especially at the holy Communion.

The practice of private prayer, Bible-reading, and self-discipline.

Bringing the teaching and example of Christ into his everyday life.

The boldness of his spoken witness to his faith in Christ.

His personal service to the Church and the community.

The offering of money according to his means for the support of the work of the Church at home and overseas.

(Canadian Book of Common Prayer, page 555)

The Canadian Prayer Book thus outlines the elements that should be considered in a personal rule of life, and leaves the individual to formulate the particular rule that may be best for him. It includes what are often described as the three elements of Christian stewardship: time, talent, and treasure. At the same time, it refrains from dictating the details of such a rule, or of imposing it on anyone. It gives a well-rounded outline of what a rule of life should contain, and leaves it to you and me to formulate our own.

Some, however, will prefer to share a rule of life with others who are working toward the same end. For them I would commend association with one of the Church's religious orders for men or women. Most of them have "associates," or a "third order," consisting of those who live in a busy world but who want to formulate a way of life that will help them live in this world as practicing Christians. For these associates the order has a simple rule, with the opportunity to report on it at intervals and to enlist the prayers and counsel of the members of the community to help them strive toward the keeping of the rule.

No weapon, secret or otherwise, can be more effective than those who use it. If the laity is the secret weapon of the Church, the clergy must learn to guide and direct it. Our task as laymen is to respond to that leadership and to share in it in accordance with our ability and opportunities. We are called upon as Christians to work and pray and give for the spread of Christ's kingdom—and especially to live as Christian men and women, to bear our witness for Christ wherever we may live, whatever we may do, and however we can. For we are signed with the sign of the cross in holy Baptism, and our vocation is to follow Christ, "to fight the good fight of faith and to lay hold on eternal life."

Notes

Chapter One. WHAT CAN WE BELIEVE?

1. John A. T. Robinson, *Honest to God* (Philadelphia: Westminster Press, 1953).
2. O. Fielding Clarke, *For Christ's Sake* (New York: Morehouse-Barlow, 1963).
3. Michael Ramsey, *Image Old and New* (Cincinnati, Ohio: Forward Movement Publications, 1963).

Chapter Two. WHAT IS THE CHURCH?

1. C. B. Moss, *The Christian Faith* (New York: Seabury Press, 1943).

Chapter Three. THE ROLE OF THE LAITY

1. The Rt. Rev. Walter C. Klein in *The Living Church,* August 10, 1935.

Chapter Five. THE WORLD IS MY PARISH

1. Ernest Southcott, *The Parish Comes Alive* (New York: Morehouse-Barlow, 1959).
2. James A. Pike, editor, *Modern Canterbury Pilgrims* (New York: Morehouse-Barlow, abridged ed., 1959), p. 57.
3. Abbé G. Michonneau, *Revolution in a City Parish* (Westminster, Md.: Newman Press, 1950).
4. Alan Paton, "Meditation for a Young Boy Confirmed," *The Christian Century,* LXXI, 41 (Oct. 13, 1954), 1237–39. By permission of the author and of The Christian Century Foundation.

Chapter Nine. ECUMENICAL CONFERENCES
AND CONVERSATIONS

1. Quoted, *inter alia,* in Norman Goodall, *The Ecumenical Movement* (New York: Oxford University Press, 1961).
2. The Rev. Wilbur C. Woodhams, circular letter; quoted by permission.

Chapter Twelve. COMMUNISM AND ANTI-COMMUNISM

1. *Handbook on Communism,* obtainable from the Division of Christian Citizenship, Episcopal Church Center, 815 Second Avenue, New York 17.

Chapter Thirteen. WAR AND PEACE

1. *The Episcopal Church Annual, 1963* (New York: Morehouse-Barlow).
2. Pope John XXIII, *Pacem in Terris* (New York: America Press, 1963).
3. The Rev. Arthur Walmsley has a good statement on the failure of church people to face up to the problem in his chapter in *On the Battle Lines,* edited by Malcolm Boyd (New York: Morehouse-Barlow, 1964).

Chapter Fourteen. THE CHURCH AND SEGREGATION

1. The Rev. James Breeden in *On the Battle Lines,* edited by Malcolm Boyd (New York: Morehouse-Barlow, 1964).
2. Gunnar Myrdal, *An American Dilemma: The Negro Problem and Modern Democracy* (New York: Harper & Row; 20th anniversary ed., 1962).
3. Daisuke Kitagawa, "The Church and Segregation," an address to the U.S. Conference of the World Council of Churches, April 25, 1963.

Chapter Fifteen. THE CHURCH LOOKS TO THE FUTURE

1. I am uncertain of the origin of this prayer; it was widely used by the Forward Movement Commission in the 1930's. It appears in this form, for example, in *Forward Day-by-Day* for summer, 1937, where it is headed "Prayer of the Chinese Church." In another form ("O Lord, reform Thy world—beginning with me") it is quoted in *This Week* magazine, September 8, 1963, attributed as "A Chinese Christian's Prayer."